The Women's Daily Irony Supplement

Also by Judy Gruen

Carpool Tunnel Syndrome: Motherhood as Shuttle Diplomacy
Till We Eat Again: Confessions of a Diet Dropout

The Women's Daily Irony Supplement

By Judy Gruen

Reno, Nevada

Creative Minds Press
an imprint of **Beagle Bay, Inc.**
Reno, Nevada
info@beaglebay.com

Visit our websites at:
http://www.creativemindspress.com
http://www.beaglebay.com

ISBN: 978-0-9749610-4-0
Library of Congress Control Number: 2006938795

First Edition
Printed in The United States
12 11 10 09 08 07   1 2 3 4 5

In loving memory of my parents, Jack and Liebe Rosenfeld.

Acknowledgments

Writing may be a solitary occupation, but transforming writing into a book is a team effort. My terrific team includes Brenda Koplin for outstanding copyediting; Uwe Stender for unflagging support and encouragement; Jacqueline Church Simonds and Robin Simonds of Beagle Bay, Inc. for their careful attention to the quality of both content and design. Very special thanks to Denise Koek, who I turn to as a first line of defense against accidentally unfunny material. Denise always makes herself available to me when I need her objective eye. If I bother her more often than she'd like, she is too good a friend to let on.

I am truly indebted to the readers of my "Off My Noodle" column for their enthusiasm and loyalty. Thanking individuals who have been stalwart e-mail correspondents is too dangerous, as I may inadvertently omit some folks, so please accept this communal, heartfelt thank you for reading, for laughing, and for your wonderful letters. They encourage and gratify me.

My husband Jeff, and our kids Avi, Noah, Ben and Yael, have never complained about the fact that I write about our lives and poke fun at our foibles and minor traumas on a regular basis. (Well, *almost* never.) You all enrich my life beyond measure. Finally, I thank the Almighty for all the blessings He has bestowed on my family and me, today and every day.

Contents

Part I:

A Woman's Home Is Her Hassle

Forward This E-Mail
or I'll Break Your Kneecaps

Since I installed a powerful spam blocker on my computer, most junk e-mail headed my way finds an ignominious end in the electronic trash. Yet danger still lurks in my in box. Several times a week I receive e-mails—from people calling themselves friends, no less—containing threats and hints of extortion if I fail to do what the sender requires.

Last week I got a real doozy. A woman I have known, admired and trusted for many years sent me an e-mail with the subject line, "You *must* read this!" This seemed more urgent than the e-mails from people like Jubukkha Mugbombaba, the orphaned son of a former president of Togo, humbly asking for my advice on how to invest the seventeen million dollars left to him by a father who was apparently too stupid to think of hiring a financial planner. It's possible that Togo is suffering a shortage of financial planners at this time, but anyone who invites a woman who barely passed algebra to give investing advice has been running barefoot in the hot sand for too long.

In any event, I opened my friend's e-mail, which predicted: "If this story doesn't move you to tears, I can't imagine what would." Duly prompted on how to respond emotionally to what I had not read yet, I tried to open the attachment. This took some doing, as this message had been sent around the world many times and much clicking was required to finally open the blasted three-hanky saga. Finally, I began to read the story, which opened with a heartwarming scene of an innocent, happy six-year-old child whose cuteness was brought into starker relief because she had freckles, playing with her friends in a park. As you may already guess, the story turns dark and forbidding, as a freak accident maims the child, who falls into a coma. The doctors hold out no hope, but the parents refuse to accept this. Thankfully and expectedly, the story ends with a miraculous recovery, and everyone with a beating heart is emotionally drained from the harrowing tale.

If the e-mail had simply ended on that happy note, people could safely go about their business. But these e-mails never end this way. Instead, the sender, who does not trust readers to arrive at their own conclusions about the healing power of faith, miracles and prayer, ends with a threat:

"Now that you have read this, you have two choices: Return to whatever you were doing as if you hadn't read this heart-wrenching story, or you can forward this to 100 friends on your e-mail list to prove that you don't have antifreeze coursing through your veins." While I am mulling over these options, I scroll down to see if there is any more. Sure enough, there is:

"If you are so cynical that you refuse to pass this story along, you will have a freak accident at 11:00 a.m. this morning, severing your right leg. No doctor, even at the Mayo Clinic, will be able to reattach it. If you forward the story to a minimum of 100 people, you will win the next round of *American Idol* and get a recording contract. The choice is yours."

Call me reckless, but I didn't forward the story. And I was puzzled that someone who took the time to write up such an emotionally riveting saga would end it with an extortion note. I continued to work, watching the clock carefully, and wondered how my right leg could be endangered if all I did was stay at my desk and not move. My dog, Ken, often nuzzles next to my leg on the floor, but even if I didn't give him a treat it was unlikely that he would sever my leg. After all, he is used to such small disappointments.

At 11:01 a.m., I looked at my legs. They were both still there. I was safe.

This is not an isolated incident. And worse, sometimes the most innocent-looking e-mails often contain the most dire threats. I have learned to remain on high alert when reading any e-mails that feature photos of dogs in bathing suits and sunglasses on chaise lounges on the beach, cats wearing pillbox hats doing the rumba, and baby chicks with pacifiers in their mouths with their wings around each other in a group embrace. These e-mails are guaranteed to wax sentimental about friendship and taking time to smell the roses, while reminding you that under everyone's hard shell is a vulnerable person waiting to feel appreciated.

These people know a thing or two about hard shells all right, because at the end, they go in for the kill: "I sent this to you because you are my friend, and friends care about each other. Please send this e-mail to five other women who you cherish (you better include me in the list) within three minutes. Do not even go to the bathroom before forwarding this e-mail, or something horrible will happen to one of your friends and you will never have another moment's peace in your entire life. You will end up in long-term therapy, addicted to Zoloft, yet still somehow unable to sleep. Your children will run away from home, your husband will leave you, and you will end up alone, watching reruns of *Desperate Housewives* for years on end. Remember, this is National Friendship Week!"

I humbly ask that all perpetrators of this electronic extortion think twice before threatening bodily harm or lasting psychological torment to people who refuse to forward these otherwise heartwarming missives. I know that most of the people in my contact data base do not want me to forward them e-mails. Unlike me, they are too busy working at real jobs. However, I am willing to pass these along now and then—to the wealthy but clueless Jubukkha Mugbombaba. Maybe he'll keep the chain going.

And if you don't forward this column to at least 500 people within the next thirty seconds, you will develop a weird and unexplainable rash in an embarrassing place.

Happy National Friendship Week!

On Your Mark, Get Ready, SHOP!

THANKSGIVING DAY

I am basting my big bird when I answer the phone and am greeted with the following: "Hello, valued customer! Please join us tomorrow for our Annual Day After Thanksgiving Shopping Stampede! Our doors will open at 7:00 a.m., when you will find savings of forty percent off already marked-down merchandise!" No matter how much cleanup remains in the morning, I consider it nothing less than my duty as a patriotic American to participate.

THE NEXT MORNING, 7:35 a.m.

I hoof it to the mall, ignoring the turkey roaster still soaking in sudsy water. I tuck my newspaper coupons in my purse, good for an additional fifteen percent off selected merchandise (power tools not included). I park at the far end of the lot, hoping to burn off that regrettable second helping of pumpkin pie. As soon as I enter the store, an overeager cosmetics worker douses me with the new Elizabeth Taylor fragrance, "Rehab." When I can see again, I take the escalator up to housewares.

8:45 a.m.

I have never seen so many people in one place at one time in my entire life. I am pressing so much flesh I might as well run for Congress. Fighting my way through this sale-hunting sea of humanity, I discover the blender advertised in the newspaper will only go on "final" ("We're-not-kidding-this-time") clearance next Tuesday, during the Ed McMahon Birthday Sale. I snap up several new cook pans for fifty percent off and drag them back to the car, wondering if I have worked off the second piece of pie yet.

9:30 a.m.

To avoid being crop dusted again by "Rehab," I sneak into the store through another entrance, but another fragrance-wielding clerk fires at me in the neck with another new fragrance, "Facelift." I escape up to the lingerie department and, looking at the manne-quins modeling thong underwear, wonder how actual human be-ings can tolerate wearing this very weird invention. A middle-aged man looks as if he would rather be anywhere else than a room where 5,000 brassieres are staring him down, but he is stuck waiting for his wife. I nearly succumb to a two-for-one offer on a bra, until I re-alize it involves a manufacturer's rebate and I still have to pay eight bucks for shipping and handling and wait nine weeks for delivery. I don't want strangers shipping and handling my intimate garments, so I move on.

10:22 a.m.

I walk down the escalator to men's wear, hunting for sweat-ers for my husband. This will provide the ideal cover when I bag the one he's been wearing for several presidential administrations and send it to Goodwill. Unbelievably, another trigger-happy salesper-son aims and fires Calvin Klein's new fragrance, "Trillionaire," at me. I buy two sweaters, even though if I wait another week, they will be reduced another fifteen percent, during the Togo Independ-ence Day Sale.

11:40 p.m.

I have hiked back to the car two more times with sweaters,

pants, slippers and two wine decanters. I don't need wine decanters but at sixty percent off, who could resist? I have hunted through the mall twice, on a mission for signs that promise fifty percent off. I amble up to the food court where I am nearly overcome by the aroma of French fries. I have coffee and yogurt and a splitting headache. The headache worsens when I see young women wearing more earrings than pieces of clothing. I think there should be a law against some of these fashions. I feel old.

1:08 p.m.

My family has called me on the cell phone eight times, wondering when I am coming home to make lunch. But I still have a dozen things on my holiday gift list. Reluctantly, I leave the food court but am drawn like a force field into the Godiva chocolate store. I plan to only inhale, but am offered a raspberry truffle sample by a cheery saleswoman who invites me to join the Frequent Taster's Club. I take my truffle and run away.

1:52 p.m.

During their eleventh call on my cell phone, one of my children reports that everyone has given up on me and they have been forced to eat leftover turkey and it is all my fault. Ingrates! They have no appreciation for my hard work at the mall, saving money for the family and buying things for everyone except me! I'd stay and watch a movie at the multiplex, but I'm too tired to decide among sixty-eight different movies.

3:00 p.m.

I make one more circuit of the store, making sure I didn't miss anything good. When the clerk tries to spray me with another new fragrance, I am too fast for her. I leap straight into a pile of handbags, and she misses. Fortunately, I am right next to Fine Jewelry, and treat myself to a pair of gold hoop earrings for half off. I bask in the glory of knowing I participated with millions of other people in The Great Post-Thanksgiving American Shopping Stampede.

4:10 p.m.

As he helps bring in packages, my husband reminds me that as a result of the recent pipe work under the house we need to really watch our spending. Instinctively, I spray him with the new cologne I bought for him, Tommy Hilfiger's "Danger." Then I put on my new earrings and start scrubbing the turkey pan, still untouched by other human hands. I comfort myself with the thought that there are only seven shopping days left till the Pearl Harbor Anniversary Sale.

Martha's Secrets to a Picture-Perfect Pokey

Freshly sprung from the federal cooler for women in Alderson, West Virginia, Martha Stewart is rested, ankle-braceleted and primed to reclaim her position as the maven of the manor house and admonisher of the abode. Though eager to get back to work at Martha Stewart Omnimedia, Martha graciously made time for a brief interview to share some of her insights on decorating and its impact on the criminal justice system.

I caught up with Martha (and it wasn't easy, now that she's twenty pounds thinner and strengthened from daily yoga sessions in the pokey) in her Bedford, New York, mansion, whose friendly and chintz-covered confines will restrict her physically for the next several months. Smartly dressed in a baby blue cashmere sweater and linen slacks, Martha reveled in the unfettered license to wear chic outfits other than prison-issue khakis. Apologizing for having her attention diverted slightly during the interview, the woman who inspires both loathing and longing for knowledge of what the heck to do with cheesecloth spoke candidly while gluing colorful Austrian crystals on the electronic tracking ankle bracelet she is destined to wear for the remainder of her home confinement. Here, unedited, are Martha's musings:

Judy Gruen: Martha, much of the public feels you skirted off lightly with only a five-month sentence for lying to federal prosecutors over the sale of your ImClone stock. Does this bother you?

Martha Stewart: No. I didn't bilk anybody, yet I performed my sentence voluntarily, which was no easy feat. Do you have any idea how scratchy 180-thread count bed sheets can be? I wasn't expecting Egyptian cotton or anything, but don't we have laws against cruel and unusual punishment?

Judy: Pardon me, but I looked up your bedding selection available at Kmart and your own Martha Stewart designs for sheets begin with 180-thread count and only go up to 250 threads.

Martha: Well *excuse* me. Look, it's one thing to design things for Kmart shoppers. It's another thing entirely to have to bunk down with them for five long months. I admit that I learned much that was sobering while in prison, and the reality of 180-thread count bed sheets is only one of them. I'll be upgrading the Martha Stewart bedding collection at Kmart as soon as possible, but probably not until I finish designing my new line of Bernhardt furniture. I simply hadn't realized what it would be like.

Judy: Some of the inmates were intimidated by you when you first arrived. One described you as bossy when you were asked to create a floral arrangement with her. Care to comment?

Martha: Look, the woman was trying to shove hydrangeas in front of the snapdragons, for Pete's sake. And she was clumping the baby's breath in such a tacky way. It just made me want to scream. Somebody had to take charge. Besides, I hardly got preferential treatment. Naturally I had requested kitchen duty, where I could have done wonders. I mean, I don't think they even know how to deglaze a pan over there, for God's sake, but they put me in charge of cleaning the administration building instead. You've never seen such a sad case of waxy yellow build-up in your life! Of course, the place shone after I was done with it, but do you think they'll keep it up now that I'm gone? (Harrumphs.) During my last week, as a goodbye present, I did a little floral stencil work over the entryway and painted it. It's really lovely.

Judy: Speaking of kitchen duty, you are reported to have lost twenty pounds while incarcerated, yet you complained that the food was wretched, full of starches and nearly no fresh vegetables. How'd you lose so much weight on a high-carb diet?

Martha: (Pausing to rearrange the crystals before gluing them to her ankle bracelet) Who could eat that slop? It was simply inhuman. Would it hurt them to offer a banana now and then? One day I led a hike for the women and we collected dandelion greens and little crabapples and made a salad. It figures they had no raspberry vinaigrette, which would have been absolute perfection, so we improvised with rice vinegar and canola oil. I confess I was so starved for real food that I've hired the chef from Le Cirque for the next several months to cook for me. Tonight we're having braised lamb chops with horseradish sauce and raspberry scones. Yum!

Judy: Is it true that you became so sympathetic to many of your sister inmates that you've offered them jobs when their terms are completed?

Martha: Absolutely. Even though I obviously did nothing wrong, I admit that it took incarceration for me to realize how many good, decent women are out there who accidentally committed a little tax fraud or witness tampering. Is that the end of the world? Yes, I'm going to offer jobs to these women, whom I now consider friends, when they're released. Except for Evelyn.

Judy: Who's Evelyn?

Martha: Let's just say she's one tough broad who I would not want anywhere near me if she were waving my poultry shears around.

Judy: Evelyn aside, you seem to have eventually won over

many of the other inmates. Were there really tears shed when you left Alderson?

Martha: Copious tears. I had brought a little class into their dreary lives, and they were going to miss it. Also, I hadn't yet finished my six-part series on how to build media empires with only twenty dollars in the bank. And I admit they had been nagging me to do a cooking series that would have taught them essential skills, such as making a *roux* that doesn't burn. With me gone, who's there to teach them that when you open a package of cheese and see it's become all blue-gray that it is *not* suddenly bleu cheese? I cried because I hadn't seen my private jet in five long months, and I'm not too proud to admit that I missed it.

Judy: Your spin-off of *The Apprentice* was a real turkey, and Donald Trump minced no words in telling you his feelings about it in an open letter, saying, "I knew it would fail as soon as I first saw it. God, what a bore." Response?

Martha: I think that few people really understand turkey and how to cook it so that it is juicy, tender and delicious, as much as I do. And mince is vastly underrated as a condiment. When I whip up my next batch of mincemeat nonesuch cookies, I'm afraid I won't be sending any to Mr. Trump.

Judy: With so many new projects, what else can you possibly undertake?

Martha: This is still very hush-hush, but I'll tell you because I'm so incredibly excited about launching my new Martha Stewart Penal Colony Living magazine. With my personal experience in lockup, I'd never run out of editorial concept. For example, I'll have a series on keeping clutter to a minimum in a six-by-eight cell; anger management techniques to offer when the guards are acting uppity or when your cellmate has just been turned down for parole; yoga positions you can do on a chain gang; and how to sneak spices from the kitchen into your bra. I'd also have articles on how to save money when all you're making is twelve cents an hour. And of course there'll be recipes for salads you can make from herbs you can safely pick from the grounds, and decorating tips to brighten your surroundings. I'll be offering Martha Stewart paints wholesale to the United States government for use in the prison system. Women's prisons in particular are in desperate need of cheerful hues, especially pastels.

(At this point I see how Martha's assiduous yoga regimen has helped her in the jug, as she has been able to simultaneously design her Austrian crystals and glue them onto her ankle bracelet while conducting the interview. I must say, I'm impressed.)

Martha: (Raising her right pant leg and showing me her artistry on the anklet) How do you like it? (She pivots, with the insouciant pride that may be the exclusive province of a billionaire.)

Judy: It's beautiful, Martha. As my grandmother, who by the way was never incarcerated, would have said, wear it in good health. Any final words for our readers?

Martha: Yes. Remember, you can perk up nearly any room by decorating ordinary switch plates with festive wallpaper, sheet music or favorite map. Also, if you discover a lipstick stain, treat it as quickly as possible with liquid dishwashing soap to remove grease, then launder as usual.

Don't Bother Me, I'm Flinging My Boogie

I have always had a low tolerance for neat freaks, the kind of people who never lose their keys, a phone bill, or a Tupperware lid. If they suddenly need to dig up a receipt for a sweater they bought four years ago, they could whip it out in 8.2 seconds. These people annoy me.

When I groused about this one day to my friend Kay, she suggested I get help from FlyLady, the patron saint of decluttering and a big proponent of tossing ancient foodstuffs with freezer burn.

"You ought to try it too," Kay declared. "Since I started up using FlyLady's e-mail reminders, I've lost eighty-nine pounds."

I gasped. Kay couldn't end up weighing more than a baked potato if she had lost all that weight. "Okay, it was eighty-nine pounds of junk from the house," she admitted, "but that still counts!"

Kay was enraptured by the FlyLady's system. "The president of the National Organization for Women isn't as liberated as I am now that my closet is cleaned and my kitchen is organized," she claimed.

Under intense pressure, I subscribed to FlyLady's e-mails. I had no idea that this would mean I would hear from FlyLady several hundred times a day, each message bossing me around with an urgent task, such as running immediately to shine my sink, clean my desk for fifteen minutes, or check to make sure my shoes and moisturizer were on. I'm not sure what moisturizer had to do with cleaning success, but FlyLady said not to question her on this.

I hated the system. In the five minutes it took for me to go shine my sink and return to my desk, I had received another torrent of e-mailed questions from FlyLady:

Did I know where my laundry was? Was it in the process of being washed, dried or folded, or was it sitting around getting mangy and making me feel ashamed of my life? (I wouldn't have wanted her to know, but the dog was napping on top of the laundry in the basket, and I saw no reason to disturb his slumber. After all, he only manages to squeeze in about eighteen hours of sleep a day.)

Had I eaten breakfast?

Lunch?

Had I planned my dinner menu yet?

Had I laid out my clothes for tomorrow?

Had I scheduled my bubble bath for the evening? (Was she joking? I couldn't even take a one-minute bathroom break without kids banging on the door and asking me to help them find their homework.)

Had I set my official FlyLady timer for fifteen minutes, and then run a reconnaissance mission around the house, flinging at least forty-six junky old things into a garbage bag? This was Major Fling Boogie Week, and FlyLady was urging us to purge our homes as thoroughly as if we were bulimics in the john.

Had I exercised?

Paid at least three bills?

Had I hugged myself today?

I broke out in a cold sweat. Who did this woman think

she was, sniffing into my laundry basket, asking buttinsky questions about the state of my sink?

I called Kay. "FlyLady's a pest," I said. "Who has time for all these e-mails? I'm getting depressed."

"You just don't get it," Kay said, while simultaneously defrosting the freezer. "She warned you in her introduction letter not to get mad at the e-mails. Weren't you paying attention? Besides, you can't give up after only one hour."

I tried ignoring the e-mails and focused instead on finishing a writing assignment that was due by noon. Unfortunately, I became consumed by the drama of some FlyLady correspondence. She sent an unapologetic jeremiad about how the only life that was truly worth living was one where we had the gumption, nay, the self-respect, to toss plastic containers that had lost their matching lids.

I left my writing and rushed back into the kitchen to throw away my lidless containers. (I had begun with twenty-six and ended up with three.) She also issued commands like a drill sergeant ("I want this trash out of your house TODAY! DO YOU UNDERSTAND ME ON THIS???") that were hard to ignore. However, she also discouraged us from slitting our wrists (blood stains can be so hard to get out!) if we hadn't yet sorted our laundry or planned our bubble baths. After all, tomorrow was another day, and I could bet my mortgage that FlyLady would buzz back in my in box, ordering me around.

Then there were the emotional testimonials from members of the FlyLady flock. One devotee confessed that instead of wearing real shoes to begin her decluttering day, as FlyLady instructs, she wore flip-flops. Wouldn't you know it, while using her new FlyLady feather duster—so beautiful it can be displayed in an umbrella holder in the living room—she fell and got a concussion. Clearly one ignored FlyLady at one's own peril.

The clock was racing toward my noon deadline and my article was not finished, but my sink was shining, and so was my face, since I think I overdid the moisturizer bit. I failed to follow her fifty-sixth instruction of the day ("Don't procrastinate!") but couldn't help it, as I was entranced by weepy e-mails from other zealous followers. They wrote movingly of how following the FlyLady system had not only released them from shame at having icky grime all over their baseboards, but had also saved their marriages, helped them switch to more favorable adjustable-rate mortgages, and released them from dependence on antidepressants. One discovered that her husband really, really liked those purple ostrich feathers on the duster, and not just for swabbing lint from those hard-to-reach ceiling fans, either!

Still, I quit the FlyLady program after three days, because the woman was giving me a nervous breakdown. The house is more chaotic again, but my nerves are a lot calmer, and in the end that's all that really matters.

Oh, Just Stuff It

I don't mean to brag, but over the years my Thanksgiving turkeys have been widely acclaimed as "not too dry." And yet, I realize there's always room for improvement. That's why last week I went to a special holiday cooking class.

Naturally, the class was held in one of those huge, *Better Homes and Gardens* type homes that had a kitchen seemingly designed by Emeril Lagasse. Gleaming pots and pans that looked as if they had never seen the hot side of a burner hung merrily from a shiny chrome ceiling rack. The counters, all five miles of them, were granite, and the kitchen's center island was big enough to hold all the prisoners currently stationed at Guantánamo Bay.

My good friend and culinary whiz, Ruth, taught the class. Now Ruth is the kind of woman who would never be caught dead without a full jar of imported Hungarian paprika, fresh saffron, and a full set of candy molds. My kitchen is never without a family-sized box of Chips Ahoy and several gallons of ketchup.

During the class, I looked forward to Ruth teaching me the epicurean's way to season, stuff and slice old Tom for the holiday. But even more, I looked forward to her demonstrating how she made her famous cinnamon swirl buns and chocolate fudge cake with chocolate liqueur glaze. I knew from previous experience that these classes were not spectator events, and I couldn't wait to sample the goods at the end of the evening.

I dutifully took notes as Ruth showed us how to make other Thanksgiving essentials: fresh cranberry relish, sausage stuffing for Uncle Tom's cavity, three different styles of yams and sweet potatoes, and Asian greens with Thai vinaigrette (this last item obviously handed down directly from the Pilgrims). Ruth dazzled me as she threw around fancy culinary terms such as "garnish," "drizzle," and "invert." And I could only dream of a day when, like Ruth, I would have five *sous* chefs standing around my kitchen, handing me little bowls of freshly grated lemon zest, chopping up fresh basil when I needed it, and instantly washing, drying and putting away every bowl and spoon I used.

Ruth was a marvel to behold. Her turkey looked as if it had spent two days sunning itself in the Bahamas, and many of us hovered over the granite counters in hushed reverence as we watched her expertly wield a poultry shears and slice off the bird's thighs. Ruth explained that this shearing "let him breathe," but given that old Tom had been cruising at an altitude of 350 degrees for about four hours, breathing seem rather superfluous at this point. Then, electric knife in hand, Ruth carved that bird in exact quarter-inch slices, each one completely symmetrical. Some women openly wept.

Finally, we got to the good part: dessert. I watched intently as Ruth tossed together the chocolate fudge cake in only one bowl. In only sixty seconds, Ruth had prepared the cinnamon bun dough, making the Cuisinart do her bidding. Even the steel blade on that machine didn't dare get dirty when Ruth commanded the buttons! As the Cuisinart kneaded her dough, Ruth explained something scientific about yeast and gluten, but I wasn't listening. I just looked at my watch, calculating how long it would be till that baby came out of the oven. Ruth glazed the inside of the dough like an artist painting with a pastry brush, demystifying the process of getting that delicious glaze to ooze right inside those buns. Now I was in on the secret, although I knew that when I tried them at home, mine would never come out as perfectly as hers.

Everything that Ruth had prepared was sublime. And yet, I left the cooking class suddenly filled with shame because, unlike Ruth, I did not grind my own fresh pepper or own a fish scaler. So the next day, I set out to claim a sense of empowerment by arming myself with the tools of a professional chef. I went to Ruth's favorite restaurant supply shop, where I discovered to my shock that there were regular people out there who actually stocked their larders with orange zest strips and wasabi caviar.

Restoring my self-esteem set me back a few dollars, but it was worth it. I spent nearly forty dollars on a pepper mill made by a foreign automobile manufacturer, and an undisclosed amount on two sets of rose-shaped mini bundt pans. My new mortar and pestle look just as intimidating on my counter as I had hoped. On my next trip, I'll probably spring for that butane culinary torch I had my eye on. Why not? If you've got a hankering for baked Alaska, I say, go for it.

Tomorrow, I'll roll up my sleeves and cook for the next two days for our Thanksgiving banquet. It will take me that long since, unlike Ruth, I don't have five sous-chefs available for the grunt work in the kitchen. And even if my turkey still comes out "not too dry," I don't think anyone will much care. Once I bring out those rose-shaped mini chocolate fudge cakes for everyone, nothing else will seem to matter very much.

When Bad Contractors Happen to Good People (A Tragedy in Three Parts)

Part I: Verily, It Is Easier to Destroy Than to Build

An old adage says that nothing in life lasts forever. Until recently I believed this fiction. But now I know differently, because we have been in the agonies of remodeling one bathroom—I repeat, one bathroom—for so long now that it's like the movie *Groundhog Day*. Each day I wake up to the same nightmare: a huge Jacuzzi tub docked like the *Queen Mary* on my bedroom floor, bits of plywood and tubs of tile grout in the gouged-out space where we used to have a bathroom, and no workers in sight.

Like Bill Murray in the movie, I despair of ever waking to a new day, when the paint chips, sawdust and empty cups from Jack-in-the-Box littering my yard are finally hauled away and it pays to dust again in the house.

My contractor estimated that this job would take three weeks, yet since this "minor" project began, postal rates have increased twice, and I watched as a Costco warehouse (only slightly larger than two football stadiums) was erected from the ground up just a few miles from my home. I have played hostess to a veritable army of scruffy, non-English-speaking men tromping through here in work boots, wielding hammers and two-by-fours. I have begged (in English and Spanish), pleaded, and dangled warm, home-baked chocolate chip cookies and cash bribes just to get them to finish.

For several weeks it looked tantalizingly close to completion; so close that my husband and I dared to dream, "Perhaps by the weekend . . . ." Yet, like Congressional filibusters, home construction is an interminable process. Some days, progress is measured by nothing more than some new guy sauntering into the house, blasting holes in a wall, then leaving, announcing he is going to lunch. I will never see or hear from him again. Other days, progress is regressive. For example, last week a guy with too many earrings for my taste took a sledgehammer to several pieces of the just-installed, brand-new tile. Apparently, these tiles needed to be removed because the contractor forgot to tell another worker to first install some thinga-majiggy in the wall that would regulate the water temperature in the tub and shower. Though I am paying the bills, I am powerless in the face of all this ineptitude.

However, I am getting ahead of my story. Let me go back to the beginning of how I have found myself chained to the house for the past many months, peeking out the window every five minutes like a kid waiting for Santa, praying that today the spirit might move the workers to come back to the job.

It isn't as if my husband and I looked at each other one day and said, "We have too much money just piling up around here. Let's unload some of this excess cash and invite nervous breakdowns by remodeling the bathroom!" This whole sorry episode was launched after we were assaulted by the bad odor in the laundry room last fall. We hired a plumber to hunt for the source of that embarrassing stench. He rooted around under the house but found no formerly living odiferous creature. Unfortunately, he made another discovery: The entire subfloor of our bathroom had rotted away, and if we didn't do something soon, such as rip out the bathroom and build a new one, the next time we took a soak in the tub we just might find ourselves falling right through that floor and end up pole dancing with our subterranean rusty pipes. Of course, all this could have been avoided had the seal around the tub been tight, but I can't bear to go there now. It's just too painful.

As anybody who has any experience with remodeling knows, it is first necessary to find a qualified contractor. A contractor's job, once you sign the contract, is to drop out of sight for weeks at a time, eventually surfacing to assure you that he will continue to harass the workers into showing up at the job site sometime soon, maybe even in the next fiscal quarter. I managed to get several lukewarm recommendations for contractors (no one, it seems, remains happy with their contractor after any prolonged contact), and called a dozen of them. Most did not deign to return my calls. Those who did call back laughed themselves apoplectic when I told them I wanted an estimate to remodel a bathroom.

"What's so funny?" I demanded.

"No one wants to bother with a bathroom remodel. Can I interest you in a second story or sumpthin'?" And people have the nerve to complain about the economy.

I strong-armed a few into making appointments, but they never showed. Getting desperate, I called a name I picked at random in the Yellow Pages. I left a message for Roland, apologizing profusely for asking him to consider such a lowly, paltry job as mine. He called back promptly and did not laugh. I became suspicious immediately.

"Why are you returning my calls? And why aren't you laughing at me?" I asked. I assumed he must be desperate for work and no good.

"Any smart businessman knows that a small job might one day turn into a large job," he said. Perhaps because he had a nice

South African accent, which to my mind always makes someone sound intelligent, I ignored the implied threat of his statement. We agreed on a price, and my fate was sealed.

Part II: They Came, They Did Some Drugs, They Went to Lunch

After lining up Roland the contractor and Joe the plumber, I felt exhilarated. I was proud of my hiring instincts. Finally, the job would get done, and pleasantly, I thought. After all, I enjoyed Roland's charming South African accent and Joe's delightful Scottish lilt. Joe said things like, "Let's have a wee look down under the house" and also called me "love" whenever he tried to explain something about plumbing which he suspected I didn't understand, which was often.

Besides, I had come perilously close to hiring a contractor named Garth, who had no accent at all and who had been building a new porch for my neighbor. Garth seemed to do careful work, evidenced by the fact that he had been laboring on this porch for about a year and a half. He was real friendly too, greeting me cheerily each time I walked by with our dog, Ken. But when I invited him to give me an estimate on the bathroom remodel, I discovered that Garth had a disgusting habit. He announced a sudden need to tuck in his shirt, which required him to unzip his pants in front of me. I ran out of the house, hiding in the shrubbery for a half-hour, and then, mustering my courage, went back inside, praying that Garth had tucked himself in, and then booted him and his zipper out of my house. Now the dog and I walk in the opposite direction of Garth and his porch.

Before Roland could bring in his crew to demolish the bathroom, however, we needed Joe to redo the plumbing. Our pipes dated from approximately World War I, and, like muskets, gas-lit street lamps and other inventions of that vintage, it was time for them to go. I wanted Joe to do the work himself, but he sent over a lackey named Stu who talked too fast and had trouble making eye contact. I was not warned that re-piping the house would require Stu to rip out large hunks of walls in nearly every room, but Stu insisted this was the only way to access all those hard-to-reach places where my bad plumbing was hiding. Stu spent hours crawling along the underbelly of the house and then would emerge, clapping dust all over the house. I felt he took a perverse pleasure in showing me how our pipes—even the ones of newer vintage—simply crumbled like sand in his hands. Stu offered his opinion that these supposedly newer pipes had been installed by Sleepy, Sneezy and Goofy. Really, I should be thankful that we hadn't had massive leaks under the house since the pipes had been held together by Elmer's glue and pipe cleaners.

A neighbor who stopped by in time for one of Stu's rapid-fire speeches pulled me aside and said she suspected Stu was on drugs (her guess was crystal meth) but I couldn't figure out a polite way of asking for a specimen for drug testing. Of course, I certainly wouldn't have had this problem with Garth, but it was too late for buyer's remorse. Therefore, I lived with the uncertainty that the guy replacing Sleepy, Sneezy and Goofy was actually Dopey and Happy. I guess spending that much time under houses can really get to a guy.

After two weeks of Stu tearing gashes out of the walls, he announced on a Friday afternoon that he was sorry but had to turn off all the water in the house, leaving us with no working toilet or sink. Then he left for the weekend.

I tried to remain cheerful. Everyone had warned that remodeling projects never go smoothly. So far, they were uncannily right. Having several sons and a backyard meant that the lack of a toilet presented the biggest problems for my daughter and me, and my husband, who has classier hygiene standards than our boys. Over the weekend, we trudged outside to the back office, where we still mercifully had a working toilet and sink, but it was cold in the middle of the night, and the practice became tiresome.

By now alert readers will already have guessed that Stu never came back. By the time I figured this out several days later, I called Joe and told him how Stu had left us high and dry, so to speak.

"Holy mother of God!" Joe exclaimed, following this with some choice Scottish expressions I didn't understand. "I'll be right there, love!" he assured me. By the end of the day, Joe finished our re-piping job. He apologized for having sent me a drug-crazed employee but also reminded me that because we had agreed on a set price, Stu's laggard pace and excessive chattiness had cost him a bundle, too. I offered Joe a whiskey, and we parted friends.

I gave Roland the happy news that the plumbing was ready. The next morning, two guys with hammers came over at 7 a.m. and smashed my bathroom to smithereens. If this was all the skill it took to demo the bathroom, I should have had my eleven-year-old son do it. He would have done it for a Slurpee and had tremendous fun also.

Ever the cheerful hostess, I ran out and bought a dozen donuts for the workers. But when I offered them up along with a fresh-brewed pot of coffee, they said, *"No, señora. Mucho carbos para me."*

Just my luck! I got manual laborers on the South Beach diet! This annoyed me, because it meant that I, who am not a manual laborer and therefore burn far fewer calories than Carlos and José, would face the morning alone with a hot pot of coffee and a dozen donuts that I had chosen personally. Since I had to supervise these guys, I also wouldn't make it to the gym.

Roland told me that I had to go and buy thousands of dollars of new bathroom equipment, such as new tile, new sinks, new light fixtures, a new tub with an energy-efficient, self-draining, double-insulated pump, as well as obscure items like "male aerators." These male aerators were available at Home Depot on the same aisle where they sold female, bisexual, cross-dressing and transgendered aerators. This was an intimidating shopping list. Tubs, for example, come in hundreds of varieties, and I had to be careful to order the kind with the center drain and a left-hand pump to fit our new plumbing setup. Since this tub would be shipped from Outer Mongolia and would arrive in approximately two months unless I paid an express shipping fee of many hundreds of dollars, I really didn't want to have to also pay a restocking fee if I got these details wrong. Of course I paid the express shipping fee, since Roland said he'd be ready to install the tub in just a few days. The tub arrived and then sat on my bedroom floor for six weeks.

Roland took measurements and told me how much floor and bathtub tile to order before setting me loose in the tile stores. I brought home samples, laid them down on the new floorboards, and then changed my mind repeatedly. I began to sense that this project was going to eat up a lot of time. After Roland's boys finished tearing up the bathroom, they seemed to lose interest in the other part of the job, namely, the rebuilding part. I began to worry when I had to put Roland's cell number on my speed dial. Unfortunately, by that point I knew it by heart anyway.

"Roland, the guys haven't been here in three days," I said, still patient, still going with the flow. After all, this was to be expected.

"They haven't? I'll call them right now and get them over there!" he promised. So I waited, and waited, looking out the window for signs of their truck. One morning, I was excited to see their truck in front of my house, but when I went out to greet them, I saw they were sleeping. I think that's what happens when you stay on a low-carb diet for too long—you just lose your get-up-and-go.

Our bathroom thus remained in a state of demolition for several months. My tile finally arrived after being delayed in Customs (at least that's what they told me), but without the matching edge pieces that Roland forgot to tell me to order. By the time he remembered, the dye lot on the tile had changed, so I had to order edge pieces that did not match

"When will the bathroom be done?" asked my husband and kids.

"Soon!" I said, willing myself to believe it.

And each day, I did not go to the gym, because, fool that I was, I kept thinking that the workers would show up. I decided that if the situation didn't change soon, I would have to take matters into my own hands.

Part III: The Puck Stops Here

One day, when the moon was in the seventh house and Jupiter aligned with Mars, one of the workers, José, showed up again.

"Where have you been?" I said, trying to walk that fine line between gratitude for his presence and fury that he had been AWOL for a week.

José looked unhappy. "Mr. Roland, he no pay me! I take other job, but I have to finish here."

What a rube I had been! I had assumed that since I had paid Roland, the contractor, big hunks of money for the bathroom remodel, he might have been paying the workers doing the actual labor. But as my eleven-year-old likes to point out, I'm very gullible.

Desperate to keep José on the job, I shouted, "I'll pay you! Don't worry about Mr. Roland! Just work today and come back tomorrow! I give you cash!" I waved some twenties in front of him to prove my sincerity, and then wondered why I had lapsed into broken English.

"Okay, okay, you nice lady," José said. "I need twenty minutes, I finish the job."

"Twenty minutes? That's all you need is twenty minutes?" This was impossible, even for someone as eager for payment as José. Many things still needed to be installed, such as the vanity, sink, faucet, and tub. The walls needed patching, sanding and painting. I couldn't understand what José was trying to say, but after an exhausting forty-five minute game of charades, I realized that he needed some kind of wall-filler that dried in twenty minutes. I grabbed my car keys and dashed to Home Depot to get it for him.

I was so happy to have José on the job that I didn't realize what a bumbling moron he was. I couldn't take the time to inspect his work because he had me running back to Home Depot every few hours to get more materials, such as huge boards of plywood that would not fit in my minivan. Only after José disappeared (as they all do eventually) did I take a closer look at his work and realize that he had installed the bathtub tile crookedly. However, if you look at it while drunk or if you have a migraine, it looks kind of okay.

Meanwhile, my fury at Roland grew to pathological proportions. The bum hadn't returned my calls for ten days. I couldn't think of any possible excuse, unless he had been kidnapped or run over. As a matter of fact, I began to enjoy the image of him blindfolded and handcuffed. If I ever did find him, I just might run over him myself.

Roland had insisted that the tub be the last thing to go into the bathroom, and it had been sitting like a docked cruise liner on the floor of our bedroom for six weeks. I had tripped over it several times in the dark of night, wending my way around it as I fumbled my way out of the room and to the bathroom down the hall—a trip I would not have had to make if our own master bathroom had been restored to us.

The last few times I had spoken to Roland, he feigned shock that his workers had failed to materialize. This had become a predictable pattern.

"I'll be there myself at one o'clock," he promised. Like a doofus, I waited, but he didn't show up at one o'clock. Perhaps he didn't mean one o'clock Pacific Standard Time, but in Botswana.

My voice mail messages for Roland became increasingly harsh, perhaps even shrill. I wanted to fire him, but I couldn't figure out how to achieve this if I couldn't reach him. Then José let slip that he knew where Roland lived—a potentially deadly piece of information since José had dangerous tools but no payment from Roland. This gave me an idea, and I sat down to type.

"Dear Roland," my letter began. "You are a cad, and belong in the Contractors' Hall of Shame. You are, in fact, the worst kind of cad, since you have a deceptively gracious accent, and I bet that's fake, too. Your bozos have done only bits and pieces of work here, despite my feeding them donuts and freshly brewed coffee. You have taken my money and run away from the job. Don't bother calling me back [I knew this seemed somewhat silly, as the chances of his calling seemed remote at best] since I now know my way around Home Depot as well as I know my way around Bed, Bath & Beyond, which is to say, intimately. You have received your last dime from me. I'm in charge now. You and I are through, you cad."

Enjoying my repetition of the word "cad," I slipped the letter into an envelope, put on dark glasses and a big hat, and left the letter on Roland's porch. Since his car was in the driveway, I made a run for it.

Roland reacted to the letter the way you would expect a drug addict to react when told his drugs had just been flushed down the toilet: He went nuts. The moment I got home my phone was ringing. Well, at least I figured out how to get him to return my calls.

My now-former contractor was filled with righteous indignation, among other fillings. How dare I write a letter like this? Was I crazy? Did I want a lien put on my house? Anyway, how could he have returned my calls when he had been on jury duty?

"Jury duty? Where? In The Hague?" I exclaimed. You'd think he could have thought of a more original excuse than that. And so, falling for his promises yet again, I told him he had twenty-four hours to get a crew back in the house and get the job finished and the trash hauled from the yard or we were really, really through. I meant it. Kaput. Splittsville. The conversation had a disturbing high-schoolish feel to it, but it couldn't be helped.

With the prospect of money slipping away, Roland got cracking. The next morning, a platoon of new workers trooped into the bathroom, followed by the erstwhile contractor himself, who at long last deigned to grant me an audience. I did not offer anyone donuts, home-baked cookies, or coffee—not even instant. It was no more Mrs. Nice Guy.

The new crew began inspecting José's work, shaking their heads and yelling at each other excitedly in Spanish. One of them actually sank to his knees and made the sign of the cross. Something told me this wasn't good news.

"Oh man, he screw up, he screw up bad!" one worker moaned, searching his pockets in vain for a rosary. Alarmed and demanding a translation, I learned that, among sundry other mistakes, José had welded the new Roman tub faucet onto the sink. Come to think it of it, that faucet did look a mite big for a bathroom sink. This welding job presented certain logistical difficulties.

None of the other workers knew what to say. Roland looked subdued. I shot him a wrathful look. I thought about killing him on the spot, but there were too many witnesses.

"This is a job for Caesar!" Roland finally intoned, flipping open his cell phone and quickly pressing a number on his speed dial.

We waited anxiously for about fifteen minutes, listening to the odd leaking sound that the toilet now made since José had reinstalled it. While we waited, my phone rang. It was a local mortuary, inviting me to take advantage of a special "pre-need" program they were offering and a two-for-one plot sale. I quietly gave the mortuary sales guy Roland's full name and address, booked a double plot, and instructed him to bill Roland directly. Then, feeling much better, I resumed the wait for this new savior of the bathroom remodel.

Moments later, Caesar arrived. He was huge, measuring five feet eight inches both up and down and sideways. As he lumbered through the house and into the bathroom, I was sure he would loosen the new floor joists.

"Hail Caesar!" I said, waving my hands toward him for good measure. With Caesar on the job, Roland ordered everyone to get the job finished, "no matter what it took, and to get it done today." He said this several times, making sure that I heard it, and then was gone.

This was several weeks ago. Caesar did manage to wrest the Roman tub faucet off the sink, but mangled the reinstallation on the tub. He managed to correct the placement of the steam unit in the wall for the shower, but disappeared with the steam unit cover that he promised to replace. The faucet handles are set so hard that only Barry Bonds, or Caesar himself, could possibly open them. He never got the tub stopper to work, but I discovered that I could still fill the tub through the showerhead (though this took several hours) and keep the water in the tub with a hockey puck over the drain. After all, necessity is the mother of invention.

Yes, I admit to you, my friends, Roman tub faucets, and countrymen, I am now writing to bury Caesar, not to praise him. The evil things that men pretending to be contractors do live on after them; the good things are oft' interred with their empty coffee cups from 7-Eleven. Let it be this way with Caesar.

Of course, Roland never got the trash hauled away, never made sure that the work was done. But he never got another dime from me again, either. It was an empowering moment when I finally realized that I could continue to be stupid and call Roland hundreds of times and still not get the trash hauled away, or I could finally wise up and open the Yellow Pages, make one call, and get it done myself. Oh yes, it was a fine, empowering moment when I wrote that check to the trash hauler and had the detritus of the remodeling job banished.

Now I have hired a guy named Speed to undo some of the damage of Roland's ragtag retinue of reckless homewreckers. But Speed comes to work each day, and takes enormous pleasure laughing at the "knuckleheads" who came before him.

One day, the bathroom will be finished. And now that Speed is on the job, it may even be soon. Then, my only other problem will be how to fix the ugly and crooked tile job José did in the guest bathroom while he was here. I'm thinking a new look for that bathroom might be nice, maybe something in a Mediterranean blue, with a skylight, perhaps. I dunno. What do you think?

Tupperwired

When Tami invited me to her Tupperware party, my heart skipped a beat. My own Tupperware was more than a dozen years old, and while the stuff never breaks, mine had begun to look craggy and tired. In fact, it looked a lot like me. I marked the date on the calendar with a big star.

"What's a Tupperware party?" my youngest asked innocently.

"It's a party where you buy Tupperware," I said. She looked at me as if some of my brain matter had shifted and fallen down into my liver.

"You're kidding, right?" she said, incredulous. How could I explain that after fourteen years of motherhood, where exhilaration is often measured in finding "key buy specials" at the grocery store, a Tupperware party is exciting?

I counted the hours till the party. Sure enough, an unforeseen emergency involving one of the children and an unauthorized, self-inflicted, multilevel haircut made me arrive nearly an hour late. I was mad to have missed Tami's demonstration of the products. Now how could I possibly choose among such marvels as the Fridge Stackables sets, Forget Me Not Containers, FridgeSmart containers for produce, modular mates for non-perishables, antimicrobial cutting boards and ultra-thin cookie lifters? All the guests had their faces screwed in concentration inside various catalogs. They looked if they were cramming for a final exam.

I got dizzy just looking at the Tupperware towers on the

display table, then turned for guidance to the catalogs, filled with enticing color photos of approximately four billion Tupperware products, each essential for the organized home.

I sidled over to my friend, Nancy, who was studying a catalog as if she might discover the meaning of life in its pages. "Nancy, do you think I should get this set with red tops or the blue tops?"

"Can't help you," Nancy said. "I've got enough trouble deciding between the round versus rectangular sandwich keepers. I'll probably be here till midnight."

I am old enough to remember the days when the most complicated thing about Tupperware was remembering to "burp" the lids to ensure freshness. But this! This was wretched plastic excess, in Flame Red, Sunset Orange, Sunshine Yellow and too many other colors to count. Even worse, refrigerator Tupperware containers now came with two little vents that provided airflow to keep food fresh longer. To use properly we had to learn how to store carrots (one vent open) versus cucumbers (both open). I dared not ask about a mixed vegetable salad, fearing some kind of official Tupperware response, probably involving the rotating of the open vents on an hourly basis.

These products promised miracles: salads that would defy the passage of time, veggies remaining as crisp and fresh after a week as they had been on the day they were picked. Celery that you could tie into a French knot would be a thing of the past. Tami noticed my utter confusion. She tapped me on the shoulder and whispered seductively, "Tupperware will transform your life—for the better!"

Unable to control myself any longer, I started ordering Tupperware like a woman possessed. Tami wrote up my order, madly trying to keep up while trying to contain her own excitement. After all, the more I bought, the more free stuff she got. After I added three Tigger Lunch Sets to my order, she fanned herself and sat down. She was now only a salad spinner away from winning a Caribbean cruise.

I wrote a check for something close to our monthly mortgage, and went home in a daze. A week later, the UPS man arrived with many enormous boxes. Like someone with a hangover, I had no recollection of having ordered half the stuff.

Now I have enough Tupperware to store every product known to agriculture. My refrigerator is a study in blue-tinted containers of every conceivable size, my pantry a study in Tupperware hunter green. Unfortunately, I still have a lot more Tupperware than I have food. However, I have found that Tupperware keeps clean socks smelling fresh for several weeks at a time. And you don't even have to remember to open the vents.

The Taxman Cometh, but I'm Still Looking for My Receipts

L ike a lunatic, I've frizzled away two whole days in fruitless search of a blasted tiny blue bit of paper no more than two inches square. This is a vital document, because it proves that I paid ten bucks to park downtown for a business meeting several months ago. Without the receipt, I could still honestly claim the expense on my income tax statement. But do I really want to live in fear that an IRS agent might one day knock on my door (probably when I have ugly green exfoliating sea kelp mask on my face), confront me with the discrepancy on my tax records, and slap a pair of handcuffs on me? No thanks. I've read too many stories about guys ending up in the slammer because the words "tax" and "fraud" somehow ended up in the same sentence containing their names. I'm not taking any chances.

You might want to withhold your sympathy from me, much as employers withhold some earnings for Social Security taxes from you. After all, you might rightly say, this is a conundrum of my own making. If I were more organized, I wouldn't have tossed ten dollar business receipts hither and yon in file folders, my wallet, or in one of the eighteen cup holders in my car. But who among us is without filing sins, let her cast the first 1040 form. I am pretty careful about filing any papers that can save me money down the line. The problem is that many of these same documents fancy themselves as European workers: After only a few hours on the job, they saunter off for six weeks of paid leave in the Bahamas.

I suspect that millions of people agree with me that tax preparation has become more painful than tooth extraction, minus the Novocain. After all, hemorrhoids can be a one-time event, while tax season is the other "March Madness" that grips us every year. It shouldn't have to be this way. But what else can you expect with a federal tax code so massive? Even if you took every single copy of every Harry Potter book ever printed in the known universe and on Mars and laid them end to end, they would only cover Title 26, Subtitle E, Chapter 51, Subchapter H, Part 1, Section 5502 of the tax code. For those of you who are curious, this section deals with necessary applications to the government before commencing the business of manufacturing vinegar by the vaporizing process. And if you think I am making this up, you give me far too much credit for imagination than I possess.

Once, a maverick senator floated the outlandish idea to "simplify" the tax code. He thought there was no earthly reason why the entire tax code couldn't be a document that a normal human being might be able to read in only fifteen years (with occasional bathroom breaks), instead of thirty. As thanks for his inspiration, this Senator's district was instantly gerrymandered. He was never heard from again.

To understand what our income taxes are all about, we need to understand certain terms including "gross income," "alcohol fuel credit," "depreciation," and "American Samoa." Well-meaning people have tried to explain these terms to me numerous times but I still ended up befuddled and with a strange twitch in my left eyelid.

Years ago, I tried to calculate my own taxes. I tried to follow the instructions on the 1040-Not-So-E-Z Form, which went something like this:

Enter taxable income from line 39

Enter the smaller of line 16 or 17 of Schedule D

Subtract line 21 from line 20 on your cousin's Schedule R

Enter the smaller of line 15 or line 23 if it is a full moon (but not less then zero)

Subtract line 28 from line 86 from your neighbor's Schedule B

Enter the larger amount from line 23 or line 45 if married and filing jointly, or married and filing a joint instead of a tax return because you figure the government had already messed with your head quite enough.

Even if you are crazy enough to try this at home, none of your arduous calculations will matter anyway. No matter how many brain cells you explode trying to figure it out, the fix is in, and the government will conclude that you owe them at least $10,000.

I'm giving my scavenger hunt for the blue receipt another two hours, and then I'll turn it all over to the Lord and my accountant, who doubles as the Lord this time of year. And then I'm going to pop a couple of migraine pills and lie down, relieved that it's only another eleven months till I have to do this whole thing all over again.

A Plant Murderer
Turns Over a New Leaf

I am a plant murderer. Worse, I'm a serial plant murderer!

Like most other criminals, I have my excuses. It may have been the repressed memory—fortuitously recalled through recent psychotherapy sessions—of having been traumatized as a child by thorns on a rosebush that pricked my young, tender skin, drawing blood. But on a conscious level, I intended no harm to green, leafy life forms; bore no malice aforethought or even beforethought. It's just that the ivies and amaryllis in the nursery always look so winning, so pert and, well, *alive*. Believe me, I planned to maintain them in that same happy condition. I would take joy when they sprouted new leaves, and feel proud that they were, by their very existence, helping battle the problem of greenhouse gasses, or global warming, or something. Heck, it would have been okay with me if all they did was look pretty in the living room.

And what did they ask for in return? Just a little water a few times a week, a sprinkling of mulch every October and April. And, okay, some gentle wiping of the leaves to keep their pores open. Who knew that plants had pores? While they were doing their job responsibly, creating oxygen for me, I was in the process of killing them slowly through gardening ineptitude.

I wonder: While they perched in their plastic planters there in the nursery, minding their own business, did they have any sense of foreboding as I drew near? Did their own earthy intuition make them want to scream to the Boston fern next to them, "No! No! I'm too newly rooted to die!"

Someone should have issued a restraining order against me from approaching within 100 feet of any garden store. After all, I've got a long rap sheet. My intentions are good, but it all gets too complicated for me. Here's one example. The leaves of a new aspidistra began to turn yellow and fall off. Determined to save the thing, I immediately looked up plant care on an Internet gardening site. I learned that yellowing foliage could indicate too much light. Or, it might be too little light. It could have been caused by high temperature. Then again, it might have been a case of over watering or poor drainage. I might have given it too much fertilizer, or too little. It might have been the announcement that interest rates were on the rise. Who really knew? As usual, I failed to diagnose the situation in time. Another empty clay pot was added to my ghastly collection.

Sadly, I concluded that I could no longer be trusted with household topiary. First, every plant has individual needs for moisture, light, and emotional nurturing. What's more, plants also invite many threats from spider mites, mealy bugs, bud drop, and wilt (a particularly acute condition that begins the moment I put the plant in my shopping cart). Naturally, each of these problems requires unique treatments of light, gravel, insecticide, or trimming leaves at ninety-degree angles. To fight a plague of mealy bugs, I once found myself fencing with cotton swabs soaked in rubbing alcohol, but to no avail.

I finally gave up when the leaves on one of my plants began turning crispy and brown. These would have been reasonable adjectives to describe a chicken recipe but were fatal to my Goldstar dracaena. Unhelpfully, I read a study that proved that people who lived with plants and flowers were happier, more well-adjusted socially, and displayed a more sophisticated sense of fashion than their plantless pals. My sense of self-esteem, already withering, felt as if it had died on the vine.

The researchers also found that people who received flowers expressed feelings of excitement and delight (except when receiving daisies, which as everyone knows are the cheapest and least attractive flowers around). However, I wonder why the researchers did not ask the actual flowers how *they* felt about being cut from their life source and given to strangers; strangers who may or may not have even the faintest clue about how to take care of them. I would guess that the flowers would experience a heightened level of anxiety, leading to headaches. After all, why else are we supposed to add an aspirin to the water along with the flowers?

Now I am turning over a new leaf. I'm turning myself in to the nearest FTD florist to begin six weeks of community service, swabbing at mealy bugs with alcohol-soaked cotton swabs. I have also hired a British woman to plant flowers in our yard, since I believe that being British is the only qualification one needs for garden design. I myself will have restricted, supervised access to the garden, and will be allowed to peer at it from behind a large bag of potting soil.

As for houseplants, I'm going silk all the way. In fact, my first purchase looks so real that a visitor leaned over to smell the bouquet. I don't know why I didn't think of this solution before. Besides, I have never heard of aphids attacking a silk arrangement, have you?

The Women's Daily Irony Supplement

Part II:

Holidays and High Jinks

Is It Safe to Come Out Now?

I have taped a note on the kitchen table, explaining to my family that for reasons of national security and my own emotional stability, I have removed myself to an undisclosed location where I will decompress for the next several weeks. They don't know that I am really just hiding in my little office out in the backyard, so please don't blab if you run into them. I predict that my husband and kids will soon be wandering the streets of the neighborhood, looking for a home-cooked meal and some clean skivvies. That's why as an extra precaution I have added a security bolt to my office door.

I plan to stay in seclusion until I am absolutely certain that the last of the holiday guests have finally cleared out. Although it is nearly mid-January, I found another one lurking in the family room the other day, eating the last of the microwave popcorn. I can't take much more of this.

In the last weeks of December, we hosted more than 100 visitors for various holiday soirees, brunches, and a dinner party for some newlyweds. Squadrons of social butterflies trooped through our door bearing jolly spirits, good cheer and sometimes bizarre gifts, such as the singing fish plaque that turns its head and sings "Don't Worry, Be Happy!" It could have been worse: They could have brought fruitcake.

And speaking of fruitcake, one night I flipped through a *Martha Stewart Living* magazine that some thoughtless person had brought me, thinking I might relate to it. *Big* mistake. In its glossy pages, I was subjected to a smiling Martha explaining how she whips up 212 individual fruitcakes for her closest friends for Christmas and bakes them in ceramic containers that she glazes and hand paints herself. (The containers double as planters after the fruitcake is gone, naturally.) I stuffed the magazine into the trash and steeled myself to get back in the kitchen for the next batch of Duncan Hines Turtles. More guests were arriving the next day.

As the holidays wound down, the locals were relatively easy to get rid of, though they tended to leave the water running in the guest bathroom. But the moochers from the Midwest and Canada were a different story. Once they personally verified that Los Angeles really is seventy-two degrees at the end of December, they simply refused to budge. I knew there'd be trouble when I discovered two guests from Ottawa just standing outside in the morning wearing shorts and tank tops, grinning goofily. I thought they were nuts. After all, it was fifty degrees that early in the morning, downright frigid in these parts. They refused my invitation to come in and warm up.

"Why would we want to come inside?" one asked in amazement. "This is a heat wave! If this is global warming, bring it on, baby!" he shouted to the heavens, laughing in a disturbed manner. Later, the Canadians got down on their hands and knees and begged us to sponsor them as climactic refugees from sub-zero winters. I tried to dissuade them from this wild notion, attempted to scare them with true tales of Los Angeles earthquakes, traffic jams, and gardeners who just gab on their cell phones when they are supposed to be mowing the lawn, all to no avail. Then I had to bring out my big guns: I told them no more home-baked brownies as long as they remained under my roof, but I promised to ship some to them if only they would leave. It was a teary farewell when the sheriff came to boot them out and escort them to the airport.

Apparently, our house was the place to be this past holiday season. Accommodations were so tight in the area that right before New Year's one guy showed up at the front door with a suitcase. He heard a rumor that we still had one unoccupied corner of a bedroom and an air mattress available. He claimed to be a relative by marriage—who really knew? By that point I was too exhausted from cooking and entertaining to check his bona fides, so I just waved him in and pointed him to the kitchen where I still had some curried egg salad left out for lunch. Not surprisingly, he left the egg salad but cleaned me out of peanut butter cookies.

I know I can't stay in the office forever, but I'm enjoying the quiet and the sensation of not shopping or cooking. Next week I will sneak back into the house and tiptoe through the rooms, making sure the coast is clear. After all, ever since they found Saddam hiding under a rock I've been afraid that some of these freeloaders might get the same idea. Now I live in fear that one day when I least expect it I'll discover another Canadian cowering under a futon, needing a shave and a shampoo. This is not an appealing visual.

Until then, I'm staying in my "safe house" continuing to decompress. Fortunately, I brought provisions with me, including the leftover Duncan Hines Turtles. Until I polish those off, I'm not leaving.

News from the Good Ship Lollypop

At this time of year, friends, relatives and colleagues whom you never really liked and haven't seen in years are jamming your mailbox with their annual New Year's letters. These salutations are often longer than a Henry James novel and contain more cheery news than could fit on the Good Ship Lollypop. I wonder: Is any real family's life filled with so much unremitting happiness and success?

Last week I got one such missive from Ruth, a fourth cousin eight times removed. I probably have more genetic similarity to the Sultan of Brunei than I do to Ruth, whom I may have met when I was four years old. Still, our familial and geographic distance hasn't dampened her enthusiasm for keeping me posted on her family's uncanny tidal wave of success, year in and year out. Enclosed with a glossy color photo of Ruth, her husband, Sherman, their three smiling kids and Labrador, was this letter:

Dear Friends and Family,

Wow! Can the year be ending already? It seems just yesterday I wrote our last New Year's letter and told you about Sherman's winning the Ironman triathlon and his being promoted to district supervisor for Big Loans 'R Us

Bank & Trust. Honestly, I couldn't imagine that anything could top that!

But Fortune has smiled on our family again this year. Sherman's cost-cutting analysis at Big Loans 'R Us earned him a cruise to the Caribbean for the whole family. It was the trip of a lifetime! If they hadn't had all those jazzercise classes on board, I'm sure I would have come home as big as our breakfast nook! Sher's athletic training continues to pay off, and he kept the Ironman title he won last year, beating out guys ten years his junior.

I may have mentioned last year that Garth won a full academic scholarship to Duke, but in case that detail slipped my mind, Garth won a full academic scholarship to Duke. In addition to making Dean's List, he's also the youngest starter Duke has ever had on their basketball team! Not bad for a kid who's only 5'8"! Lydia is drum majorette in the high school band, and also heads the Teen Division of our neighborhood's anti-poverty campaign. Between school, band practice, and the anti-poverty campaign, I don't know how she also finds time to tutor severely autistic children, but somehow she manages. Not to be outdone, Emerson has won the National Spelling Bee (you may have seen his photo in *USA Today*). This was the first time a private school student beat those pesky homeschoolers, who had wrapped up the National Spelling Bee for several years running. You can imagine how proud we are!

I wasn't sure how much more of Ruth's letter I could stomach without needing an injection of insulin, but like a lookie-loo slowing down to see a traffic accident, a perverse curiosity drove me forward. I continued reading.

As for me—Ruth rattled on—the government finally granted my patent on an herbal-based skin cream that does everything that Botox can do, only without freezing your facial expression. And to think I came up with the idea while pruning our garden! (You may recall that our garden was featured in an issue of *Metropolitan Home* as an example of what you can grow in a small space.) Now that I have secured investors, I'm hoping to take my new company public sometime next year. I must say I'm pretty excited!

Finally, we can't neglect our faithful dog, Gastro. After extensive research, we found a suitable female purebred Lab whom Gastro could "get to know," in the biblical sense. The results are seven adorable Lab pups that fetched top dollar! Gastro will also appear in a new book featuring dogs in comedic situations. He will star on several pages, including one where he looks "doggone" dashing, donning sunglasses and a visor!

I hope the New Year brings good things to all of you. Remember, you can always catch up on our family news and see new photos of us on our Web site, tooperfectfamily.org. I look forward to hearing from all of YOU!

Ruth signed off just in time, because by this point if I saw another exclamation mark I think I would have gone into a diabetic coma. I considered Ruth's invitation to write about my family's news. But how could I compete? Still, my family was nothing to be ashamed of, and I sat down to type my own end-of-the-year summary.

Dear Friends and Family,

The Gruens are closing out this year in much the same way we did last year: The garage still needs clearing out, the toilet in the guest bath still doesn't flush quite right, and I really do mean to fix that this year since it sometimes causes anxiety among visitors. Once again the family business nearly lost its lease and this caused much nail-biting, but fortunately the landlord was indicted on tax fraud and while he's in the slammer our lease automatically renewed for another three years, so we are sleeping easier at night.

We were honored in a manner of sorts by the local library as the patrons with the most overdue books and heaviest fines. They even took a picture of us holding a pile of overdue books and hung it up in the branch for a whole month. Some folks from the neighborhood even began to recognize me in the grocery store. It's not fame, exactly, but it's nice to be recognized nonetheless.

I also received a record number of rejections from book publishers. However, I don't plan to rest on my laurels and certainly plan to top this number in the coming year. Everyone knows that the most successful authors of all time boast of having collected hundreds of rejection slips before they made the big time. I'm just making sure I cover all my bases.

The kids are doing swimmingly as well. We received far fewer phone calls from the school principal than in previous years and the boys have logged fewer hours in detention, so we are clearly moving in the right direction. I'm pleased to report that during our last dental visits everyone in the family was found to have less plaque than they had previously. We are one family taking our gum health more to heart (if you can excuse the mixed metaphors). Also notable this year: Our youngest took the bold step of agreeing to eat a green vegetable, and her essay, "The Secret Life of Plankton," was published by the fifth-grade newspaper. We are, as you can imagine, quite proud.

I stopped to review my letter. My family's achievements were so lackluster compared Ruth's family's plucky accomplishments, but in my opinion over-achievement is overrated. Too many Type A's flame out too quickly, having had no experience dealing with adversity. Slow and steady wins the race, I always say.

I had exhausted myself trying to think of more impressive highlights of our year, so I took a break to get some vital projects done around the house. After clearing the garbage disposal of a plastic bottle cap and cleaning the hamster's cage, I felt a renewed sense of accomplishment (perhaps the type that eluded my distant cousin Ruth) and got back to the computer to finish off my letter.

In addition to several new writing projects, my goals for the next twelve months include finding an auto mechanic who will finally find out why the car keeps making that awful rattling sound when I put the gear in reverse, and making an appointment to have a family portrait taken. I realize that if I continue to wait until everybody is out of braces, some of us may be in dentures. To think that the youngest didn't even have teeth when we took the last professional photo is, well, kind of embarrassing.

In short, nothing extraordinary happened this past year, and for that I am grateful. No one is sick, in jail, in the nuthouse, or on the street. The kids may sometimes have attitude, but they don't have tattoos or body piercings, at least none that I have seen.

Wishing you all a terrific New Year!

I mailed my letter to a few friends, and even to Ruth. But I made up a new return address on Ruth's envelope with a big fat arrow, so she would think we had moved. This was my only assurance that I wouldn't receive her next letter, in which Ironman Sherman would no doubt have become governor of their state and Ruth would have made the Fortune 500 list.

Now I'm off to check my mail. Wish me luck that today it's only bills and catalogs.

The Gift-Giving Blues

When our newspaper delivery guy slipped his annual Christmas card in the plastic sleeve hugging our paper, I tucked the card in a very safe place. After all, the man had taken the trouble to share his home address in case I was moved to reciprocate my own heartfelt greeting, secured by some U.S. Treasury greenbacks. I play along every year because I value my newspaper, and do not want to search for it behind the overgrown bougainvillea each morning. When I misplaced the card, panic washed over me. Now I'd have to set my alarm for 4:30 a.m. to catch the guy and deliver his Christmas payola.

This example neatly sums up the problem with holiday gift-giving: There are precious few gifts that are completely innocent of subtle extortion, desperate expectations, political motivations, or terminally bad taste. Thinking about this has afflicted me with an aggravated case of the gift-giving blues. It may not sound serious to you, but trust me: night sweats, nausea and dizziness are not merry.

We all have a gallery of regrettable gifts. My worst one arrived back in college. I was heartsick over a failed romance (another in a series), and a rabidly feminist friend and very first real gay person I ever met wanted to cheer me up. He knocked on my door, gave me a sympathy hug, and then handed me a book called *Battered Wives*. His sincere smile told me that he considered this seminal title on the subject of domestic violence just the thing to lift my spirits. It was at that moment that I decided to become a humor writer.

All kinds of gifts can zing and sting. One year, my friend Deborah received an outfit several sizes too large for her. "Is that how she saw me?" Deborah wondered in despair, before shucking the clothing. Many people unload bad or duplicate gifts by "re-gifting," but this carries its own dangers. Few have absorbed this bitter lesson better than me. Years ago as a bride-to-be, I received two tea kettles. I thought it was sheer genius to re-wrap one of the kettles and give it to my friend Sharon, who had spent a lot of time helping me prepare for my wedding. My ego swollen with unmerited feelings of altruism, I presented Sharon with the tea kettle. When my smiling friend pulled out a card inside the kettle, I knew I was done for. I hadn't put a card in there, which meant that the card was addressed to me. My re-gifting scheme was about to be nakedly revealed.

In one horrible instant, I went from self-importance to a desire for self-immolation. I stammered my excuse, but the damage was done. To Sharon's eternal credit, she did not make a tempest of this teapot, and remains my friend to this day. But this experience was so mortifying that I have never dared re-gifting anything to anyone, even if the re-giftee lives in Katmandu. You just never know.

Now I think I know why they call the day after Thanksgiving "Black Friday." Some say it's because on this opening salvo in the Christmas shopping season retailers begin to turn a tidy profit for the year. I think it's because innocent, unsuspecting Americans are about to suffer a blitzkrieg of handmade, gluten-free muffins from Vermont; tea cozies knitted by the disabled sent to people who microwave their water; wines sent to recovering alcoholics; and pomegranate salt scrubs to folks who are fragrance-intolerant. People eager for a book that is "uproariously funny" will instead be sent a book that is "unflinching and harrowing." No American is safe. (Private message to my agent: the Mont Blanc pen I sent you for Christmas has nothing whatsoever to do with the fact that I'm still waiting to sign our next publishing deal. Nothing whatsoever.)

And yet, I would hate to give up on presents as a concept. Giving and receiving can still be exciting, heartwarming, and fun. But it's hard to find the right thing for people in a country where clutter-control storage units and professional organizers have become nearly as big a business as McDonald's. Not even my kids can think of a thing they want for Chanukah. All they said when I asked what they would like was, "Cash is king, Mom." I've proven no easier as a potential giftee. My eleven-year-old daughter asked me what I wanted, and I told her the truth: collagen treatments. But how would she wrap them?

I have solved part of the problem of holiday gift giving by buying myself an extravagant piece of jewelry. I figured it was the least I deserved for traipsing through crowded malls, doing the yeoman's work of finding everyone's holiday gifts. My jewelry is still on layaway, a paycheck away, but I can hardly wait to give it to myself. It's my consolation prize for not getting the collagen.

As to the rest of the family, I'm still praying for inspiration. With the clock ticking, they'll probably land those greenbacks they're hoping for, and some I.O.U.s for nights out together. At least that's something they really can't lose.

Families: The Gift That Keeps On Giving

Yesterday our family eagerly awaited the arrival of relatives who flew in from out of town for a holiday visit. Yet unbeknownst to us, while we were merely expectant, they were expectorating, coughing, sneezing and wheezing. They were carrying more weapons of mass infection than you could shake a thermometer at, and arrived on our doorstep with stockpiles of antibiotics, vaporizers, cough lozenges, and other medicinal balms, not all of which were covered by insurance.

We discovered this the hard way. No sooner had I flung my arms around Aunt Phyllis to plant an enthusiastic kiss on her cheek when I was met with a monsoon of micro-organisms.

"Don't kiss me!" Aunt Phyllis warned, one tragic sneeze too late. "Harrgh, oh my, ugh, harrgh, *harrgh!* I'm so sorry! I didn't mean to cough all over you! I felt so sorry for those poor people sitting next to me on the airplane. I was hacking all the way from Hackensack to Houston. I hope I didn't make them—oh oh, ugh, *HARRGH*—sick!"

I began to wonder about our national airport security. Why are these uniformed personnel, who are responsible for our safety in the skies, confiscating tweezers for goodness' sakes, yet waving others through who are smuggling contagion across state lines?

Unfortunately, Aunt Phyllis was not the only symptomatic relative who came bearing the gift that keeps on giving. Out of nearly fifteen relatives, most had some nasty disease-causing agent that set off alarm bells in pathology labs.

I had prepared a brunch, and despite the pestiferous pathogens flying around, everyone ate heartily. In this family it takes a lot more than borderline pneumonia to put the kibosh on anyone's appetite. Conversation, such as it was, went something like this:

"Ah-*choo!* Pass the fish, please."

"You just sneezed on the cole slaw. Be more careful."

"Has anyone seen my inhaler? I thought I left it on the coffee table."

"With this bad cold I can't really taste anything you made, Judy, but I'm sure it's good. Please pass the bagels."

"I think Marilyn just tried to say something. What did you say, Marilyn? Speak up!"

"She can't speak up. She's got laryngitis, remember? Everyone be quiet! What did you say, Marilyn?"

"She said to pass the cream cheese, and does anyone have some extra-strength ibuprofen?"

"Aren't you supposed to be watching your cholesterol, Marilyn? Well, here it is anyway. I won't snitch to your doctor. *Uhgchhchchch. Chchchchchugh!* Thank God that phlegm is finally coming out! Sorry, everyone."

"Who's ready for cinnamon buns?"

Admittedly, this ambiance of affliction was not what I had hoped for, but how often do we get a chance to share special moments like this with family members who live across the miles? When everyone was sufficiently tanked up on food and pharmaceuticals and the door handles were disinfected (at least for the moment), all but the most infirm among us went for a stroll in a nearby park. This exertion proved too much for some members of the party who were on medications whose warning labels clearly stated: "May cause drowsiness when strolling through parks." No sooner had we returned home when I heard the first faint rumblings about dinner. What was I serving, and when?

Meanwhile, any member of the family who hadn't been ill up till that point began spiking fevers or collapsing with chills. In-laws and kids took to our beds and couches, covered with blankets. This was no longer a family reunion; it was a MASH unit. I ministered to the minions of the miserable like a modern-day Florence Nightingale, and did what came naturally to me: I wondered with some eagerness how many calories I was burning while running from patient to patient, bringing cups of hot tea with lemon.

I sent my husband out to find surgical masks, and while he was gone the clamor for dinner became louder. This made me feel feverish, as I could not cope with serving another meal. In a flash of inspiration, I whipped out a tool from my home emergency kit: the take-out menus from our new favorite Chinese restaurant. I dealt the menus like cards at a Vegas casino and told everyone to circle their choices, like patients do in the hospital.

Immediately, the entire family began to revive. Two kids, hot-cheeked with fever for hours, rose from their beds as if from a stupor and agonized through glassy eyes over the choice between Kung Pao Beef and Szechwan Garlic Chicken. Even Cousin Jenna, fresh from foot surgery, discarded her crutches and walked miraculously to the table to join in the deliberations.

An hour later a smallish man laden with two enormous bags of Chinese food tried to get through the front door. It wasn't easy. I quickly rushed to put a surgical mask on him before he stepped over the threshold of our infirmary while the kids surrounded him, clamoring for the chicken fried rice. Even Marilyn found her voice again and asked through a throat lozenge, "Did you remember the hot and sour soup?" I tell you, you'd think that Jews had never seen Chinese food before. I put Uncle Doug to work sorting out the dozens of identical white take-out cartons, matching the right entrée with the right patient. It was not an enviable task.

I doubt that when Chinese people are ill, they say, "If only I had a hot pastrami sandwich and a bowl of matzo ball soup I'd feel so much better!" No. When they are sick, they sensibly stick to miso soup and a little rice to tide them over. Somehow, though, Jews are insanely wild for Chinese food in sickness and in health. It sounds sacrilegious, but we consider Mongolian Beef a balm even better than chicken soup. And yet, the Jews and the Chinese are both ancient peoples who have survived for thousands of years despite massive infusions of MSG and corned beef. It kind of makes you wonder if MSG and corned beef can really be so bad.

Dinner was a success, judging by a notable decline in mealtime expectorating and sneezing. As people began to depart for the evening, I gave them each a surgical mask as a party favor to wear when they would return the next night for another dinner.

In the meantime, I've got to disinfect the house again and am tending to three sick relatives who refused to leave last night. That's because they're my kids and they live here, strewing dirty tissues and banana peels about the house. Luckily, I managed to hide some leftover Chicken Lo Mein in the fridge. It's my own personal stash, and I hope no one finds it. Frankly, I'm going to need it to stay well for the duration of this family visit.

My Big Fat Sleek Chanukah Present

On the first night of Chanukah, we followed family tradition and lit our menorahs in front of our living room window. Newly recovered from illness, I had not even shopped for gifts for the family. Even in my most febrile dreams I would never have imagined that within minutes I would hit the holiday mother lode.

We had just kindled our lights when our eldest son's cell phone erupted with its standard "ring": a guy screaming something unintelligible followed by badly played rock 'n' roll. Even though I've heard it a hundred times, I get scared each time that blasted phone goes off. He flipped open his phone and ducked outside to take the call. This was the first in a series of odd events that occurred in rapid succession that should have struck me as strange, yet none registered in my befogged brain. Moments later, someone drove up right in front of the house in a brand new car, festooned with a giant red bow on top.

"Look!" I said. "Someone's getting a new car for Christmas!"

"That car looks just like the one you almost bought last summer, except for the bow," one of the kids noted. I hardly needed reminding that six months earlier, we were on the verge of signing on the dotted line to buy a new car to replace my old heap of battered steel. But giant, surprise expenses reared their ugly heads, and my plan was foiled. I still couldn't wait to dump the wrecker, with its constant shake, rattle and roll. I pined away silently for a new, sleek vehicle.

I couldn't imagine who among our neighbors had scored such an unbelievable holiday present. Why, none of them needed a new car more than I did! Why didn't they at least have the courtesy not to park this gleaming new set of wheels in front of my window? I did not think that any number of Chanukah latkes—even with generous dollops of applesauce and sour cream—could salve the pain.

While in the midst of swelling jealousy, my husband, normally a reserved sort of fellow, began singing "Happy Chanukah to you!" to the tune of "Happy Trails." This was beyond irritating. I was staring at a gorgeous car that wasn't mine while my husband was oddly breaking into song, like in a Broadway musical.

The driver of the new car, who had been just sitting in the driver's seat till now, finally opened the door, and my heart skipped about five beats. The driver was our son, which led even me (so slow on the uptake) to one electrifying conclusion: *That car was mine!* My husband had placed the phony cell phone call, cuing our son to hightail it around the corner and bring the car to the front of the house.

My husband was still singing, but I was too stunned to respond. I heard our youngest son, who had been studying first-aid class in school, say, "I hope she's not in anaphylactic shock. Her first trip in the new car might have to be to the hospital."

"You got me a *car*?" I repeated dumbly, laughing and crying. Somebody pulled me up from the couch and we all dashed out to examine the most amazing Chanukah present I have ever received or will probably ever receive in my life.

"Didn't you hear me singing 'Happy HONDA-Kah, to YOU'?" my husband asked. For a moment, I wondered if the man was launching a midlife crisis. He has no history of throwing surprise parties or sneaking up on me with joltingly extravagant presents. Was he hiding something? Under the circumstances, who could blame me for having a tough time going from expecting nothing at all for Chanukah to receiving a gift that seats eight and has cup holders for twenty-four? I'm not sure what the engineers were thinking by giving each passenger three cup holders, since the car has no toilet facilities, at least none that we have found.

I slid behind the wheel and took the family for a spin, marveling at the car's novel and dazzling qualities: Brakes. Shock absorbers. Working turn signals. Electronic everything. Individual seat warmers, for God's sake.

I drove around town all week with the bow on top, even though it was raining and the rain soaked the ribbon, which dribbled on me in the driver's seat. As if I cared. At the gym, I burst with the news about my unbelievable Chanukah present from my unbelievable husband.

"Now I need to be nice to him for the rest of my life," I said, worried about how to pull off this kind of marital trick.

"No you don't," the instructor said. "The way I see it, a new car buys him a month of being nice. If you need to be nice longer than that, he needs to buy more gifts."

"I don't think he even gets a month," noted a very pretty, very young, and overly toned young woman. "I think he gets a week. A man can never do too much for his woman."

Hoo boy, I thought. I didn't envy these women's boyfriends.

After I finished calling all my friends to tell them about the car, I opened the phone book and began calling people I didn't know, purely in the spirit of sharing holiday joy. I kept that up until I reached a woman who expressed what I considered an unseemly interest in my husband.

Driving in a smooth new Mom-mobile with a red bow on top was a real kick. Many drivers were nicer to me, going so far as to let me into their lanes. Pedestrians smiled and gave me a thumbs up, or yelled "HAPPY HONDA-KAH!," reflecting the message festooned on the top of the windshield. The big bow also helped me spot my car in crowded parking lots—it's the most festive global positioning system I've ever seen.

Some folks just looked confused when they saw the car with the bow, or perhaps they thought I was loopy for driving around with it. They were right, of course. I was so happy I *was* loopy, not just because after more than thirteen years I had a new car that promised to be reliable, but because my insanely busy husband took the time and effort to surprise me with it. After all, *you* try to find a red bow the size of a tractor wheel in town in December. It isn't easy.

Even in sluggish L.A. traffic, the car keeps me plenty busy. Time passes quickly when you are playing with the control panel, adjusting the rear defroster, tweaking the temperature on my seat warmer, and searching for cup holders. So far, I've found six more. Gridlock was never so much fun.

Big Bill's Birthday Blast

It's not every day that I am e-vited to a birthday party promising to feature live ammunition. In fact, as a mild-mannered Jewish gal with little contact with NRA members, I had never been invited to a shooting party at all. Excitedly, I e-sponded with a resounding "yes." Paula was throwing this Wild West-themed shindig for her husband Bill's birthday. It was a "BYOF" (Bring Your Own Firearm) affair, and last I checked my utility cabinet, the only thing in there that went "pop" was a bottle of sparkling cider.

"Don't worry," Paula said. "Dale and Pete are bringing extra guns and they said they'd share." That was a load off my mind. In my view, there's nothing worse than people who won't share their toys at a birthday party.

However, I had a second dilemma: We were expected at a wedding that same afternoon. I decided to ditch the wedding early, since people are getting married left and right around here, but when would I possibly get another chance to lock and load a Glock nine millimeter? The most dangerous thing I had ever handled in my entire life was a screaming, kicking toddler. I was ready for a new, bold adventure.

My husband lacked my enthusiasm for our up-close-and-personal visit with artillery, so I had to drag him from the wedding early. I smoothly navigated us in the new car over to the range. It was located in a seedy part of town, next to an adult bookstore.

It dawned on me that I was entering a different society altogether when I arrived at the entrance, which welcomed all comers with a sign declaring, "Kung Fu my ass. Try to karate chop a bullet." This sentiment definitely cleared my sinuses and I hesitated a moment before pushing through the door. A guy at the counter made us sign a very long, pesky agreement that we wouldn't do silly things like shoot from the hip, point a loaded weapon at anyone, or sue the management if we accidentally met with the business side of a gun. I signed away on all eight pages, and then tried to bolt through to the range, where I saw Paula, Bill and our friends firing away, but I was stopped again.

"Hey! You're going to need a pair of these," the man said, pointing to a pile of ear muffs. Not eager to argue with an experienced gunslinger, I slapped a set over my head and finally got into the range, where I immediately jumped in terror at the sheer decibel level of a dozen guns going off at once. My heart thudded wildly with each shot. I squeezed the ear muffs tighter against my poor ear drums, but all that did was squish my earrings against my earlobes, causing me pain. I told myself to get a grip. What had I expected? Plastic water pistols? Our friends greeted us, and the birthday boy, sporting a Luger .38, was grinning from ear to ear. He seemed to be saying something, but I couldn't hear anything other than the rat-a-tat-tat of live ammo just a few feet away. Ammo shells were popping and ricocheting, landing near my feet. If I had known it would be this dangerous, I would have brought my Kevlar vest. I was still in high heels and formal attire from the wedding, literally dressed to kill.

I had never known that our friends Dale and Pete were marksmen, nor that Dale's wife, Nancy, a sweet, quiet mother of two young children, who might weigh ninety-five pounds wearing a dress made of sand, could make Swiss cheese out of any target within 100 feet. Her daddy had taught her to shoot at the age of ten. Boy, the things you learn about people you thought you really knew! Dale showed me how to hold, load and aim his .38 semiautomatic. He clipped a fresh target paper on a reel and sent it back about fifteen feet. The target displayed a masked gunman holding a hostage.

"Okay now, that guy with the gun has just broken into your house," Dale said. "The hostage is one of your kids. Go get the S.O.B."

That was all I needed to hear. I took aim, fired, and shot off a hunk of the ceiling. A lot of good I'd do in an emergency. I'd be a lot safer if I just moved next door to Dale and Nancy. I aimed again, lower this time, and got about two zip codes closer to the dirt bag on my target. By the time I emptied the round, I had clipped his shoulder and right knee. It was progress.

I stepped back to let my husband have a go at it, and was suddenly aware that the five individuals not in our party who were shooting in their own lanes were total strangers to us. What if they were mentally unstable? What if one of them had just been dumped by a lover? What if, God forbid, one was a disgruntled postal worker? *What the blazes were we doing here, anyway?*

I was eager for my next turn and tried not to think about these other, disturbing possibilities. More ammo shells were pinging all around me on the floor. In the meantime, Paula sidled over to me.

"I hate guns," she said. "I can't believe I'm doing this at all."

"Love can make you do strange and terrible things," I yelled, since our ear muffs made normal conversation impossible.

"I'm just waiting for the pizza and beer part. That'll be a lot more fun," she promised.

I wasn't sure about that. I was itching to try Dale's shotgun, which he soon put into my newly gunpowder-stained hands.

"Gee, this is heavy. Someone could really get hurt with this thing," I said.

"That's the idea. Now let's have another go at the bad guy." Dale clipped a new target on the reel and helped me position the gun against my shoulder. "Watch out for the recoil," he warned.

I steadied the gun, aimed, and fired. The recoil, as promised, was terrific, instantly bruising my shoulder. Amazingly, I got within the target, and my friends applauded and hollered. I began to turn to take a bow but Dale screamed, "Don't turn the shotgun! Put it down!" I obeyed his command, gently laying the gun down, muzzle toward the range and away from my friends. Then I took my bow and resumed firing, with Dale photographing the moment for posterity. When I emptied it, not much was left of my target. Dale reeled in the target and showed it to my husband. "She's a better shot than you are. I wouldn't piss her off."

"I just bought her a new car. Shouldn't that buy a man a little security?" my husband asked.

I hate to admit it, but I enjoyed the sensation of holding a smoking gun. I imagined that I was ridding the world of terrorists, barbarians, and even a few low-life contractors, the kind who make you beg them to show up and finish the kitchen. But of course they never show up again. All they will do is destroy your plumbing before leaving the state. Besides, in real life, so many of our goals are moving targets. That's why holding a gun, aiming, firing and getting the shot was cathartic. The firing range management understood this and therefore promised that its beginner classes would deliver "euphoric rushes of energy combined with inner peacefulness—much like yoga." I think this gives yoga entirely too much credit. After all, you don't have to stand on your head when firing a gun.

Our kids joined us at the pizza party after, where I proudly showed off my bullet-ridden target paper to the oldest teens.

"Your mom's a good shot," Dale warned them. "Better keep your room clean."

The male ego being a fragile animal, I refrained from boasting that I had proven a better shot than their father, but it was an empowering thought all the same.

I'm thinking of going back to the range for a couple of those shooting classes, to give me that euphoric rush that grocery shopping seldom delivers. Who knows? If this writing thing doesn't go anywhere soon, I can become a security guard, and write my memoirs while safeguarding the bank. Or maybe, for my mid-life crisis, instead of entering a deep depression, I'll become a sharpshooter, join the NRA and move to a state that allows you to carry a concealed weapon. No one will know why I will have a smirky "make my day" expression. But I'll owe it all to Paula and her e-vite to Big Bill's Birthday Blast.

I've Got a Secret—
and So Does Everybody Else

I thought I had struck social gossip gold when my friend Paula let slip a delicious bit of intelligence straight into my eager ears. Paula and I were participating in a real-time, interactive social dialogue (meaning, we were on the phone) trying to schedule a lunch date. This was no easy task, as we are modern women who live the type of chronically busy lives that become grist for oodles of "how-to-simplify your life" type of books and articles that we, being so busy, have no time to read. Paula consulted her PDA and ticked off the days she was not available.

"Monday I can't take a lunch break, Tuesday I've got a doctor's appointment, Wednesday I've got a business lunch, and Thursday's out since I promised to shop with Barbara for a wedding dress."

"Barbara?" I asked. "Barbara's engaged?"

"Omigod," Paula said. "I cannot believe I said that. And I was sworn to secrecy!"

"You know you can trust me," I said, immensely satisfied at suddenly finding myself In The Know. Inexplicably, Barbara had remained one of our social set's most eligible singles for a long time. News that she was about to don the lace veil was the most thrilling information I had heard since I learned that our very nasty neighbor's pipes had burst.

"You can't tell anybody," Paula said. "But the engagement is going to be announced in synagogue this Saturday. Boy, are people going to be surprised!"

"I'll make sure to be there, and don't worry. CIA agents couldn't drag it out of me, unless they threatened to drag me to some secret detention center in the Czech Republic."

Though Paula and I failed to find a single day anytime in the following six months when we were both available for a midday sandwich, the conversation was still a rousing success by my standards. I walked a little taller (which is a novel feeling, as my kids are now so big that in my entire household I am only taller than the dog) just knowing something juicy that almost nobody else in the world knew.

An hour later, the phone rang.

"Make sure to come to synagogue on Saturday," Mimi said. "There's going to be a *big* announcement." Her "I've-got-a-secret" tone irritated me. I thought I was the only one, other than Paula and the groom, to know about the hitching. And I had kept my trap shut. I had suddenly tumbled from the social gossip elite, and I didn't like it.

"Yes, I've heard," I said, in a studied, nonchalant tone.

"How?" Mimi demanded. "Nobody is supposed to know."

"Well, you know, and I know also. Why are you calling people if it's supposed to be such a secret?"

"I don't want to deprive people of the chance to be there when the news breaks," she said. "This is *big*."

"Have you also alerted CNN and the *Los Angeles Times*?"

"No need. Larry already works for one of the wire services. It'll be known worldwide once services are over," Mimi said.

The same day, I got an e-mail from Barbara herself. "I know that Paula spilled the beans," the bride noted. "But please don't tell anyone else. I really want this to be a surprise."

"Don't worry," I replied. "I wouldn't tell anyone even if I was promised the jumbo jackpot of the California lottery, which I believe is up to forty-eight million dollars now."

As a woman of my word, I kept mum. But the next day in the market, I bumped into one of the synagogue staff. "You didn't hear this from me," he said *sotto voce* near the tomatoes, "but there's going to be a big announcement in services on Saturday. Only thing is, I can't tell you exactly what it is. Wish I could," he said, clearly relishing the presumption that he knew something that I didn't.

"Somebody already beat you to the punch," I said. "I learned about this three days ago," I said.

"Three days ago? That's impossible. This news is hot. At least that's what I heard." He sounded hurt.

I shrugged. "What can I tell you? As Ben Franklin said, 'Two can keep a secret, if one of them is dead.'"

Over the next few days, I received no fewer than four phone calls, three e-mails, and two unsubtle hints accompanied by winks about the big bombshell that was supposed to have remained a bigger secret than the Manhattan Project but had leaked like a New Orleans levee.

Barbara e-mailed me again. "I'm not accusing you of anything, but it seems that news of my engagement has already traveled round and round. I only accidentally told twelve people, and they each promised not to breathe a word of it. Only two days left till the announcement, so please restrain yourself from passing the info any further."

At that moment, the king-sized down duvet that I planned to get for Barbara as a wedding gift shrunk to a three-speed blender. I may be a writer, but I'm no leaker.

On Saturday I arrived at services early. The place was standing-room-only, a very rare condition. It was as if God Himself had been announced as the guest speaker.

When the prayers were over, the rabbi stood to announce what by now was the worst-kept secret in the history of Western Civilization. The women were all on the edges of their seats. Two even slid off.

The air in the room was electric, as the rabbi dropped hint after hint about the identity of the bride and the groom. Finally, to great fanfare, he announced Barbara's engagement to a man whom most of us did not know. Not that it mattered. Two more singles had been rescued from the cauldron of singles events, blind dates, wretched dates, and Internet dating services. We sang and danced as if we had just discovered and trademarked the recipe for world peace, or least the recipe for a good nonfat cheesecake.

It was still one of the best secrets, if not the worst-kept ones, that any of us had ever heard.

Post-Bar Mitzvah Stress Disorder

Our youngest son has just celebrated his bar mitzvah, and I am recovering from a case of Post-Bar Mitzvah Stress Disorder. This is a seriously under-reported malady, yet shockingly, the government has yet to allocate a single dollar to research. If this doesn't change soon, I'm going to launch an awareness campaign, complete with blue and white ribbons, pins and car decals.

Post-Bar Mitzvah Stress Disorder (PBMSD) usually follows a case of Pre-Bar Mitzvah Stress Disorder. This is characterized by speed-dialing your caterer several times daily until you actually hear him chewing antacids while you speak; zipping around so frantically from errand to errand that you have no time to eat anything other than large brownies in the car (perversely, this still causes weight gain); and bursting into tears with no warning because your little boy is no longer a little boy but a newly minted teen who has the audacity to catapult into puberty before your very eyes.

You don't need to be Jewish to understand PBMSD. After all, symptoms are identical to those that flare up after other life cycle events, the kind of life cycle events that often demand throwing large parties for people, some of whom are not on speaking terms but who will be forced into close proximity with one another for several hours while having to smile during much of that time.

My symptoms became acute as the weeks counted down to The Big Day. The following diary entries explain why:

Five weeks before the bar mitzvah: The invitations arrive, but the envelopes won't seal shut. Wrestling the envelope flaps down with a hot glue gun for six hours eventually does the trick. I struggle to pare down guest list, and fail. Like a powerful Hollywood party hostess, I withhold a batch of B-list invitees, pending the acceptance rates of other guests.

Four weeks and counting: Son is still growing too fast to buy the suit. He practices his Torah chanting each night, perfecting the reading. I worry about his speech, since the boy talks ninety miles an hour. Is it too late to hire a speaking coach?

Three weeks to go: Response cards coming in each day, many including checks. Son discovers that happiness is a positive cash flow. An alarming ninety percent of invitees have accepted! Cannot decide about B-list. Send to all anyway.

Two weeks left: Son has grown another inch and still afraid to buy suit. In meeting with caterer, son insists on a dinner menu of corn dogs and pasta. Fortunately, few thirteen-year-old boys are on the South Beach Diet. Musician calls me repeatedly, urging me to hire his entire orchestra. I repeatedly refuse, citing budget concerns. This is not a presidential inauguration, I tell him. It's just a bar mitzvah. Musician sounds dirgical. I remain firm.

One week and a half away: I help son polish his speech, restraining myself from over-editing. We simply add a few transitions and a laugh line or two when appropriate. Son's delivery speed still faster than a major league pitch. Consider speech printouts on each seat?

Seven days away! Musician, magician, and caterer all need deposits. Consider asking son for loan.

Six days: Should I get a new dress? Daughter and many female friends are asking what I plan to wear. I had planned to lose ten pounds for the occasion, but failed to take necessary actions. Too late now! Decide to wear ivory-colored spring suit, which still fits. Musician calls again, countering with an offer of just one additional musician. I agree, just to get rid of him. The fraud detection department of my credit card company calls to warn me of an unusual amount of activity on my account.

Five days: Must get son's suit now. Even if he grows another two inches this week, it will still fit. Son insists all formal shirts in the store are too scratchy. I snag a hand-me-down shirt from the closet, worn at an older brother's bar mitzvah. Finally, I save money!

Four days: Try to pre-arrange seating for family dinner. No configuration seems likely to prevent Uncle Harold from starting up with Cousin Norman about . . . what was that fight about, anyway? Pray that Aunt Shirley takes her meds before arrival. Stock up on my supply of migraine pills . . . just in case.

Three days: Call everyone who hasn't sent in response card. Some remind me testily that they did send them in and I must have lost them. Of course they are coming! Several of son's friends call to ask me if I can arrange their rides to and from the party. I lose my house keys.

Forty-eight hours: Caterer calls and says he can't get the special petit fours I had ordered, and a trucking strike on the East Coast may mean we can't get the sorbet, either. Default to bakery cookies. Photographer calls. An emergency has arisen, and she'll send her trainee instead. Will that be okay?

Twenty-four hours: I supervise floral delivery to synagogue.

Florist with heavy Italian accent assures me they will be "stupendous," but doesn't warn me they're as big as Mount Sinai and won't fit through the door. At home, the phone won't stop ringing. Everyone apologizes for calling, since I must be so busy, but what time is the party called for? Can they bring a niece who unexpectedly flew into town? Two invitations are returned as "address unknown." My keys have not shown up yet, and I lose my spare set as well. Next move: climbing through the window to get into the house.

The Big Day: Get up early enough to put in contact lenses and dress with care. On goes the ivory suit. While drinking a quick cup of coffee in the kitchen, a crisis erupts. The dog rushes in from the yard, ecstatic at seeing me after an absence of four-and-a-half minutes. He leaps up to greet me, festooning my ivory suit with muddy paw prints. I've got to leave for synagogue in three minutes or I'll miss son's big moment, but have no Plan B for another outfit. I race to my room and throw on a dark blue suit whose jacket won't button all the way. No one seems to notice, so like a dope I call attention to the unnecessary fact to my friends.

Son chants his portion from the Torah beautifully. He looks both adorable and handsome in his suit, straddling that brief, shining moment between boyhood and manhood. Miraculously, he delivers his speech slowly enough for most people to hear, and waits as I had instructed him for the congregation to laugh at appropriate moments. Ah, the sweet satisfaction of seeing that, sometimes, nagging really does pay off. In his speech, he thanks his father for taking him to Dodger games; me for correcting his grammar. He is in his glory, and I am in mine, even if my dress is too tight.

Four days later: The party goes smoothly. Some computer glitches make the music intermittent, and the silences are hard to explain. Several people wander into the hall, fill plates with food, and leave. I have never seen these people before in my life. The desserts are a big hit, especially the brownies. I could have told them that. Keys still MIA.

Five days later: My son's fifteen minutes of fame are over, and he is returning to life as a mere mortal. He announces his first major purchase with his bar mitzvah money will be a chameleon and a six-month supply of meal worms. He also announces plans to grow his hair very long. And each day, he continues his deployment into manhood, standing a little taller, his face and body becoming ever thinner. The next time I see his chubby cheeks, they'll be on my grandchildren. I am wildly happy that he is not embarrassed to say, "I love you, Mom."

His dad and I are immensely proud of him, and love him more than any words can say. I am also nearly wildly happy that my keys finally turned up—in the backyard. My symptoms of Post-Bar Mitzvah Stress Disorder are dissipating at last.

Only twenty-one months till my daughter's bat mitzvah . . . .

Seven Romantic Tips from Gals Who Really Packed Heat

In a few days, men will be jamming floral shops across the country, quietly cursing the extortion of Valentine's Day. In my single days, I was too naïve to realize that the men I saw carting candies and flowers through the streets on February fourteenth were not displaying any spontaneous outpouring of love for the women in their lives. They were acting on a primal survival instinct warning them that if they dared appear at home empty-handed on Valentine's Day they were facing several nights of solitary confinement on the couch.

Do not mistake Valentine's Day for a real holiday, such as Superbowl Sunday or National Lactose Intolerance Awareness Day. February fourteenth is like a Congressional tax hike—loved by those few who reap the cash but despised by most, especially by single women without boyfriends. This is a day that used to plunge me into an abyss of wistfulness—not to mention an assortment of Mrs. Smith's strawberry, apple and chocolate cream pies. And, while married now, I have not forgotten my single sisters out there, on the brink of heart-shaped candy madness.

Recently I began to wonder: Who was Saint Valentine? How did he catapult himself, along with billions of pounds of praline-filled chocolates, into eternal fame? Diligent research on the Internet revealed that Saint Valentine was a priest, but don't jump to any impious conclusions about him yet. The emperor who ruled during Valentine's lifetime required a large army, and he also believed that single guys, with all their pent-up energy, made better soldiers than married guys. Logically, the emperor outlawed marriage for young men. But the sentimental Valentine defied this order and continued to marry off young couples. Later imprisoned for his disobedience, Valentine fell in love with his jailer's daughter, even sending her a fateful letter signed, "From your Valentine."

Is any of this true? Who knows? Who cares? The point is, candy and flowers are a poor substitute for the extravagant, emotive gestures of some of history's greatest, most fabled lovers. For example, Anthony fell on his sword after hearing a rumor that Cleopatra had overdosed on eyeliner and died. Sadly, falling on one's sword is no longer fashionable, having given rise to the newer fashion of morose and bitter lovers complaining of their fate on the *Montel Williams Show*. More's the pity. If done correctly, falling on one's sword for the woman you love is pure gallantry, though messy. As for Cleopatra, I can't imagine what she was thinking. Any woman brave enough to allow a snake to chomp at her neck would also have been brave enough to brush herself off after losing a lover and peruse the photos and descriptions of possible new lovers via an online dating service.

Not to be outdone, Shah Jahan built the Taj Mahal in the Seventeeth Century to memorialize his favorite wife, Arjumand Banu. Sure, the guy built one of the Seven Wonders of the World for her, but isn't that the least a man could do for a woman who bore him fourteen children? Still, one must credit where it's due. I'm hard pressed to think of too many men nowadays who would be willing to hire 20,000 workers and 1,000 elephants to build anything nearly as grand, what with liability and workers' comp insurance being so pricey these days.

I'm willing to bet that Frank Butler never forgot when Valentine's Day came around, either. He met his wife, Annie Oakley, when she showed up to accept his challenge to beat him in marksmanship. Butler first laughed at the notion that a young woman could out-shoot him, but it turned out Annie was carrying more than one concealed weapon: After she beat Butler at his own game, he fell in love with her. Once they married, Butler managed her career for several decades as she performed in Buffalo Bill's Wild West Show. He also did the manly yet sensitive thing and died eighteen days after Annie fired her last shot.

Of course, February fourteenth is a fine day for romance, as long as the romance doesn't seem artificially induced. Even lit candles and glasses of Chardonnay aren't always enough to stoke the fires of romance, especially if you have managed to get two parking tickets that day and the fever of love has given way to feelings of anger at local government. Fortunately, archeologists have just unearthed an ancient self-help manuscript on how women can excite passion and ardor in their men. In a remarkable coincidence, the manuscript seems to have been a collaboration among Cleopatra, Arjumand Banu, and Annie Oakley. Here are a few of their suggestions:

1. When your man comes home from a hard day of waging war against infidels or shooting hard-to-catch bison, don't blather on about how the dryer repairman kept you waiting for three hours. Instead, offer him a tasty drink that requires a photo ID to purchase if you appear to be under thirty years of age. Serve the drink wearing only your six-shooter. It doesn't matter if you're heavy with child (again) and feel self-conscious dressed this scantily. Your man will love it. After two or three drinks, your man will love anything.

2. Before you go out for an evening's entertainment watching lions eat Christians, don't ask your husband trick questions, such as, "Does this toga make me look fat?" Men hate questions like this. They never know the right answers. If you think the toga makes you look fat, and your sweetheart rushes to assure you that it doesn't, you may accuse him of not being observant about your appearance. And if you think the toga is slimming, why bother asking him? Reserve all questions about which clothes make you look fat for your girlfriends, who, unlike your husband, are paying microscopic attention to these matters.

3. If your man says in an offhand way, "I'm thinking of invading Outer Mongolia and becoming its despotic leader. What do you think?" Favor him with the dewy-eyed look that you have perfected to an art form and tell him you think it's simply genius, and that you're so proud to be married to such a daring visionary. Then quietly check your important papers to see how much life insurance he's carrying.

4. If your man's five o'clock shadow has morphed into a scraggly beard, don't complain. Sidle over to him with a bowl of water, some shaving cream and a razor and tell him you miss seeing his handsome face. If necessary, remind him that you are indeed a better shot than he is, and are carrying his thirteenth child as well.

5. If hubby is in the mood for love, but seems to be emitting either a strong curry breath or an aroma that can only be described as *eau d'horse*, offer to walk with him down to the river to freshen up. Make sure to tell him it's only so that you can observe him in his natural state.

6. When you have a major purchase in mind, such as a new fleet of chariots, be smart about timing the conversation. Cook his favorite meat for dinner (venison is always a good choice) and wait till after he's imbibed several glasses of an adult beverage. Ask him

how his plans are going for the invasion, while stroking his beard, which has grown back. Slip into something more comfortable, and take him to the boudoir. When he is exhausted and nearly asleep, casually mention your plan for the new chariots. He'll probably murmur something vaguely resembling "yes," and you'll be good to go, girl. This is always a winning strategy for sensitive topics.

7. Finally, if your man ever forgets your anniversary, birthday, or Valentine's Day, a non-verbal reminder is best and least threatening. Place your calendar on the table, and draw a large sad face in the square of the forgotten day. Next, nonchalantly set out your Glock .45 automatic and begin polishing it in his presence. Unless he's had one too many adult beverages, he'll probably skip right out to the nearest quarry and start ordering marble for your next Taj Mahal.

Judy Gruen's Semi-Realistic New Year's Goals

Generally speaking, I don't make New Year's resolutions. Why should I? I'll just end up breaking most of them and then feeling shoddy and shallow, woefully lacking in discipline. But goals are good things. We need them in order to inch our way toward a more meaningful life, or at least one where we don't misplace our keys so often.

Since "resolution" sounds utterly too solemn, these are my semi-realistic New Year's goals. That is, they will prove to be semi-realistic if I don't blow too many of them too fast, but I am banking that the potential shame of failing to meet them, after I have declared them publicly, may keep me more honest.

My first goal is to try to make more time for the things that are important, not just for the things that are urgent. Work always seems urgent, while friendships, reading, and thinking get put on the back burner. Nearly every day as I take my kids to school I drive past the home of one of my closest friends. Each time I see her house I wonder how life has become so frazzled that we barely have time to see each other. A few days ago, I called her from the car to see if she had a half hour to spare. She did, and in a much-needed shot of spontaneity we had breakfast together. This was fun, but more than that, it was important, because she is my friend, and I treasure her friendship.

One of Erma Bombeck's best-selling books is titled *Families: The Ties That Bind . . . and Gag!* It isn't easy living with multiple personalities, especially when some of them all happen to inhabit the same body. This year, I will also try to express to my kids that even though they leave drawers open, drop their laundry on the floor, pretend that they don't hear me when I tell them to get cracking on their homework, tease the dog, and sometimes behave as if their only goal in life is to inflict lasting emotional damage on their siblings, I still love them with all my heart. I'm going to hug and kiss them more often. Especially the teenagers.

I am going to write little love notes for my husband more frequently than at the end of every fiscal quarter. He deserves it, probably more than the kids. After all, he doesn't even tease the dog or drop laundry on the floor.

This year I will stop pretending that I will ever give up chocolate. On certain days, chocolate is one of my four major food groups. I am about as likely to give it up as the Pope is likely to convert to Judaism, despite that suspiciously Jewish-looking skullcap he wears. Besides, my husband's grandmother just turned ninety-five and she eats chocolate every day.

In another example of hope triumphing over experience, I will try to become more organized and not lose so many things, especially my elegant new Cross pen. I bought myself this gift in a fancy pen shop, even though my track record in the area of holding on to nice pens is pathetic. It feels so much nicer to write with a "writing instrument" than a cheaper-by-the-dozen job that leaks ink on the side of my hand and on the paper just when I have finished signing my name.

I'm planning to spend more time sitting in our little garden, just enjoying its beauty. I hope that one day I can develop the same excitement and awe that my friend Diane has when she looks out on her garden in her Seattle home. I have always admired the way Diane continues to marvel at the daily miracles of a dahlia bursting forth in dramatic purple, or watching shoots sprout from a passion flower vine. These "small" everyday miracles are gifts from God. I want to take a few minutes more each day to savor them.

This year, I will refuse to feel intimidated when I receive magazines suggesting sixty-eight New Ideas to Simplify My Life. Who can possibly hope to absorb so many new concepts in one sitting? The very thought of it fatigues me. I'll just close my eyes and point randomly at five or six ideas and hope to get those right.

I am going to try to spend more time thinking about the things that matter and less about those that don't.

I'm still on the hunt for a really good moisturizer, especially one that can deal with fine lines around the eyes. I'm open to suggestions.

I want to make my work matter, my words count for the good, and to spread a little good cheer along the way.

I plan to schedule in more time for God and for prayer, thanking Him for all His blessings. As a wise person pointed out, our relationship with God isn't all that different from our relationship with people: If we make Him important to us, He'll make us important to Him. Our lives are certain to be richer for it.

I wish you all a healthy, happy, prosperous and blessed new year.

Part III:

Magnificent Obsessions

Clutched by Purse Fever

Unless you have been orbiting in a NASA space shuttle and thus shielded from earthly fashion trends, you know that designer purses have been the absolute *bon ton*. This was of no concern to me until I realized that my fifth-grade daughter had become purse-crazy. When I caught her pronouncing the name Louis Vuitton with a perfect Parisian accent, I knew things had gotten out of hand(bag).

I tried to discuss this with her but she was surfing Internet stores, ogling a profusion of purses so expensive she'd need a lifetime's worth of allowance to afford one. "Oooh, look at this Dooney & Burke!" she gushed.

"Why do you care?" I asked. "You're only ten years old. The one purse you have has Winnie the Pooh on it!"

"Mom, signature purses are the in thing. Don't you know?" She shook her head in resignation. Just her luck to be born to a mom who buys signature-less purses at off-price retailers. But my daughter was determined to educate me about these café society, *über*-chic bags, so off we went to the mall.

I admired a smart black Burberry in Macy's but could not touch it, as it was locked securely behind a glass case. By craning my neck I could just make out the price. "This purse costs $650—and it's on clearance!" I sputtered. Living in a retail world anchored by Sears on one side and Kohl's on the other, I was in a state of shock.

My daughter rolled her eyes: "What did you expect? Come on!" She pulled my hand and we strode purposefully to a Louis Vuitton store. Of course, our only purpose was to gawk, but such was the price of mother-daughter bonding. When we stepped into the hushed reverence of the store, I was alarmed. My vast experience as a consumer had taught me that generally speaking, the denser a store is populated with merchandise, the cheaper the goods. I shop at stores where clothing is mashed together so tightly I must use a small crowbar to dislodge the hangers to get at the goods. But in the Louis Vuitton store, I saw no merchandise at all. I presumed that the purses on the wall were some kind of museum collection, hence the armed guard at the door. Then I realized with mortification that these rarified pieces of baby blue suede goatskin and ostrich leather *were* the merchandise. The rest of the naked store was meant to intimidate, with its presumption that only the great unwashed of humanity shopped in places with actual merchandise splayed hither and yon on the premises.

Using their retail radar, the two elegantly dressed saleswomen sensed immediately that I was way out of my league in their cash-cow confines. They sized me up as an interloper and exchanged furtive looks that conveyed the withering message: "She shops at Target!" They tried to hide their contempt, but, being French, they failed.

"May I help you?" asked one woman, whose makeup was marvelously applied. My daughter tugged at me and whispered, "Don't ask anything stupid, Mommy!" Suddenly, I felt a righteous indignation. How dare the saleswoman presume that I would *not* plunk down obscene amounts of money on a purse! Her first clue might have been the cheap pen marks on my own handbag. You simply don't allow these things to happen to purses crafted from crocodile leather.

I politely asked to see a handbag enthroned on a gleaming glass shelf. She showed it to me reluctantly, never quite letting go of it entirely. Despite my own palpable fear of sullying it with my plebeian hands, I took it from the woman and examined it. It was painfully obvious that if I had to ask how much something cost in this place, I couldn't afford it. But I couldn't resist asking anyway.

"This one is $770. The matching wallet is $440."

Without stopping to process my thoughts, I blurted out, "Is it hard for you to say that with a straight face?"

"Not at all," she said. I thought I heard her grind her teeth. "These purses are all handmade in Europe." Well, if they were making that many francs sewing purses, no wonder they were knocking off after a thirty-hour workweek. "Besides, this is our more affordable line. Purses in our limited edition *Trompe l'Oeil Fabuleux* line sell for more than $7,000 and there's a waiting list to get them. Not ten minutes ago Uma Thurman left the store with the last one I had in stock. Now that Uma's got one, the waiting list will become months long." She sighed. "If you saw it, you'd understand. It's extraordinary."

This was not the first time that Uma had beaten me to the punch with a fashion statement, and frankly I was getting tired of it. "I'll just add my name to the waiting list. . . next time I'm here," I said, fearing that I might suddenly collapse in a heap of bourgeois humiliation. "Thanks for your time." The saleslady smiled smugly as my daughter and I beat a hasty retreat.

We devoted the next hour pretending to have a serious commercial interest in Farragamo bags that are ironically called "hobos" and cost $600. When is the last time you saw a hobo toting around a $600 purse? For the first time in my life, I carefully examined Kate Spade, Coach, and Dooney & Burke bags. They were beautiful, except for the orange ones, and certainly unlikely to have the zipper break a week after purchase. Many came with lifetime warrantees, care-and-feeding instruction booklets, and Lloyd's of London insurance policies.

In the Coach store, I inquired of a far nicer sales clerk if she thought someone dressed like me could pull off carrying around the Coach Bridle Classic Enamel Tank or the Hamptons Houndstooth Satchel without causing the public to mock me.

She furrowed her brow in concentration. "It depends how daring you are. And how badly you crave public approval," she answered.

"Tell me," I asked, appreciating her candor. "Why do middle-class women splurge on purses this expensive?"

"I have no idea, but they bust their bank accounts doing it. Of course," she added, "they are magnificent, aren't they? They're not your cheapo twenty-five dollar designer knock-off."

"Indeed they are not!" I laughed, as I slipped my own twenty-five dollar cheapo designer knockoff around my back and out of sight.

Our foray into the world of private label purses, clutches, satchels and wallets unnerved me. Until my daughter had brought it to my attention, I was happily oblivious to these purses for princesses. But now that I had seen them up close, I felt myself falling into the dangerous clutches of purse envy. I began to rationalize: Just because I had to fly coach, could I not carry Coach? What kind of law said that only film stars could carry Farragamos? Could only Kate Moss carry a Kate Spade? I begged to differ! It was not beyond my means to buy such a specimen of purse, though it would force me to nip into my offshore account in the Cayman Islands, which I was loath to do.

I tried to nab a bag bargain on eBay, but gave up when the best deal I could find was a "Sexy Violet Hermes Birkin Bag" for the astonishingly low price of $12,499. Other Vuitton bags were a paltry $7,000-$8,000, but the seller warned me to act fast, as supplies were limited.

I wrestled with the decision of whether to pop for a chic tote. But I stopped when I realized that even a $250 bag, pretty much the bottom of the barrel in these things, really would end up costing me much more. A signature purse would require a complementary signature wardrobe. Otherwise, it would just look sloppy. Updating my wardrobe would take at least $10,000. And a glamour purse would also require glamour wheels. I'd have to dump that old Ford and get a Range Rover to make a really smashing ensemble. That would set me back another $80,000, not including taxes and dealer prep charges. Naturally I'd have to ditch all my cheap pens so they wouldn't bleed over the fine satin inside my purse. A proper, upscale pen would cost at least $40. I was sobered by the thought that accessorizing my purse would cost me $90,290. Frankly, I could buy 3,612 of my regular cheap purses for that kind of dough, and I can't imagine needing any more than 1,500 throughout my lifetime, even if I live to 100.

The next day, I was delivered from purse lunacy by a museum catalog that landed on my doorstep with the mail. There I found a fine tapestry bag embroidered with books all around. It had a roomy interior and cost only a fraction of a Coach. Okay, so the lining was polyester, not satin, but the straps were real leather. If I couldn't look like Louis Vuitton or Burberry was my bag, at least I could look literate. Best of all, this bag didn't have a waiting list, and I'm pretty sure I'll have mine before Uma Thurman gets hers.

I can't wait to get it.

Releasing My Inner Shopper

My kids had accused me of being out of shape, but now I have put that vicious canard to rest. Yesterday I displayed the stamina of a professional athlete competing in the unappreciated sporting event known as the Shopathon. In this event, I stormed every inch of an outlet shopping mall the size of Houston in less time than a Nigerian can run the Boston Marathon, and still returned to a normal resting pulse rate within two minutes.

Truthfully, I would have preferred to shop at leisure rather than like a crazed lunatic, but it was the price of admission to the mall. It began when my husband announced unhappily that he had to drive all the way to Camarillo—a full hour from our home—to visit a client. This statement immediately triggered my retail radar: I suspected that this client, who managed a retail clothing store, was located in the enormous Camarillo outlet mall, populated with an alphabet soup of consumer emporia, from Anne Klein to Zale's jewelers.

My husband is allergic to shopping, so I didn't tell him of my suspicions. Instead I consoled him, "I'll come along and keep you company. And while we're there, we may as well pop into that outlet mall nearby. You really could use a new pair of shoes." I tossed this last part in with studied casualness, not daring to reveal my secret ambition to release my inner shopper. This is because this man's position on shopping is maddeningly narrow. Like many of his sex, he mistakenly focuses only on the flow of money out of our wallets and into the wallets of people who are not us. As a result, he utterly fails to tap into the excitement of bargain hunting, the discovery of a new powder blue sweater with a perfect jewel neckline, or the feeling of accomplishment that is the natural and just reward of fueling the national economy. Why has the hunting-and-gathering instinct that had served men so well throughout history somehow been diluted in modern man?

Despite sky-high gas prices, I ensured that we took the van on the trip, knowing full well that our small car could not possibly contain us, two kids, and the loot I imagined hauling away. We found my husband's client smack in the heart of the mall, with stores as far as the eye could see in every direction. Be still, my heart! I handed out maps of the place, and studied mine assiduously, as if searching for the Lost Ark. The family then dispersed to their respective missions.

"Meet back here in an hour," my spouse said. "I don't want to waste the whole day in a mall." This time limit was as draconian as it was wildly implausible, but he didn't need to know that yet. When my daughter and I had high-tailed it away from him we both laughed out loud, asking God to make sure that his meeting would be lengthy and drawn out.

Our initial goal was to shop for shoes, yet we never saw the inside of a shoe store. This was hardly our fault, as we were continually distracted by consumer obstacles. These included a discount cosmetics store selling my favorite makeup, a fine china outlet where I picked up a serving dish at forty percent off the department store price, and a gourmet chef store, where I stocked up on wedding gifts.

"You seem like you're in a hurry," the clerk said as he wrapped the gifts.

"We're shopping with a man who hates shopping," I explained. "Time is short. If he comes in here looking for us, we weren't here. Got it?"

He nodded knowingly. "Mum's the word," he promised.

We dipped into Harry & David to sample some fresh-brewed coffee that I found overly nutty, then dashed back to reconnoiter with our next of kin. The meeting had ended, but happily, my husband had apparently absorbed the festive air of commerce. He even agreed to devote another half-hour to finding himself new slacks and a pair of shoes.

"That's very wise," I agreed. "Everyone should buy themselves new clothes every fifteen years or so, whether they need them or not." No one pointed out the obvious, which was that it was nearly impossible to even cover the distance to the store in a half-hour, let alone try on clothes and pay for them. Still, guys are sometimes capable of weird feats like this. The thought sent a shiver down my spine.

As the Gruen guys headed for guy stores, my daughter and I made another attempt at shoes. But in a display of elder abuse, she yanked me forcibly away from Vitamin World, where I was considering a bottle of flaxseed oil on clearance. I wasn't sure what flaxseed oil was supposed to do for me, but it sounded extremely healthy.

I insisted that we stop "just for a second" in Geoffrey Beene, testing my frustrated daughter's patience. But then we hit pay dirt: As I paid for two sweaters, we were handed coupons for five dollars off at Van Heusen that would expire in a half-hour. Eureka! My husband was headed toward Van Heusen! Excitedly we called his cell phone, but he didn't answer. Hearts pounding, we flew out of the store, our purchases banging against our shins. Breathless, I called him again once inside the store.

"Where are you?" I demanded. "I can save you five dollars at Van Heusen!"

"I'm already at Van Heusen!"

"So am I!" I looked up and saw that we were speaking to each other from fifteen feet away. (The cell phone reception had been remarkably clear, come to think of it.) I tossed the coupon at him and bolted toward the Gap. Athletically speaking, I was somewhere between optimal aerobic heart rate and cardiac arrest, and my shins were bruised. Still, I did fifteen repetitions of bicep curls with my heavy bags, while still running. Some people looked at me strangely, but what did I care? Some of them were shopping with small dogs in pet strollers. Who were they to judge me?

My credit card was in a state of nervous collapse, but I was invigorated as if I had been drinking in mountain air for a week. Worried that my husband would call a halt to our shopping, I turned off my cell phone. If he really wanted to drag me away from the mall, he'd have to find me first!

Unfortunately, he found us, and we were forced to cease and desist from shopping. I looked forlornly at a frozen yogurt shop, thinking that if anyone deserved a big schooner of peanut butter and chocolate yogurt it was me, but I could no longer press my luck.

For all the traipsing I had done through a dizzying number of stores, my personal booty only amounted to two sweaters and one eye shadow. This seemed to lack a certain justice. All other purchases were for family members and friends, which only proved beyond any doubt that shopping is not the vacuous, selfish endeavor so many people accuse it of being. It is worthy, noble, and selfless. And sometimes, it beats the pants off spending an hour in the gym.

Back in the Saddle Again, and Boy Am I Sore

There are few finer or more sublime experiences than cozying up during cold winter evenings with hefty servings of old-fashioned, fattening food. (They don't call it "comfort food" for nothing.) But these dreamy food fests can exact a nasty price, specifically, discovering that after a week or two of this behavior, your entire wardrobe has shrunk, and in some cases, by a whole size.

When this happened to me, I wasted one whole hour doing deep relaxation exercises in preparation for stepping on the scale. That's when I realized that sucking in the gut while being weighed does nothing—nothing!—to reduce the hateful number. Whoever claimed that broken chocolate chip cookies didn't have as many calories as whole cookies was, tragically, wrong.

I decided to do penance. The most severe punishment I could conjure was attending a spinning class at the gym—wretched physical labor if ever it existed. The fitness industry doesn't want this to get around, but when those torture chambers were discovered in Iraq, they found two dozen recumbent bicycles and a whole slew of CDs filled with the mindless techno-crap "music" they play in spinning classes. And yet, we Americans can still learn a thing or two from this. Why not sentence our most hardened criminals to fifteen years in the nearest 24-Hour Fitness, where the only activity would be spinning classes? No college education, no making license plates, just spinning, all day, every day. I bet you the entire federal deficit that those ne'er-do-wells would finally understand what it means to get tough on crime.

While I loathe and despise spinning as exercise, I couldn't argue with the opportunity of burning a whopping 400 calories in an hour. I straddled the only bike left unoccupied in the spinning class. Fortunately, this was located in the back of the room, so that few people would notice, and perhaps pity, the unsightly panty line showing through my Spandex pants.

Melissa, the instructor, was already barking confusing instructions: "Give me thirty seconds in a two o'clock position!" "Now raise the resistance and give me sixty seconds in a four o'clock position!" I never caught on to the subtle differences between where our rusty-dustys were supposed to be at two o'clock versus four o'clock. Mine would have much preferred to have been on the couch while I savored an Edith Wharton novel. But I had to deal with reality, so I just kept fiddling with the resistance lever, hovering between full aerobic capacity and cardiac arrest.

Adding insult to injury, Melissa kept asking, "Are you all feeling *great*?" It was a presumptuous question, not allowing for alternate responses. And the class was well trained. They whooped and hollered in response, raising their water bottles for a collective, self-congratulatory swig. Melissa drank from a jug big enough to have filled my minivan's tank for a week. Frankly, I suspect the spinners just made those whooping noises because no one was capable of forming actual words.

Despite the caterwauling, spinning remained so boring that I attempted a little friendly banter with the woman next to me. She already had a great figure and was spinning her little thighs into oblivion. "You aren't really enjoying this, are you?" I asked, lowering the resistance lever yet again.

"In a kind of masochistic way, I suppose," she laughed. "Hey, does your back hurt?"

"No. Am I doing something wrong?" I began to worry.

"It'll probably hurt tomorrow," she promised.

The seconds trudged forward in agonizing slowness. My legs were spinning, but my mind felt leaden. At one point I thought I heard Melissa order us to "move our ovaries" but I was too embarrassed to ask my neighbor if that was what she really said. Anyway, even if Melissa had commanded me to move my ovaries, I couldn't exactly expect mine to oblige just on her say-so.

Although my legs could not rev around as fast as many of my spinning comrades, I outlasted the weaklings who pooped out, some as much as fifteen minutes early. Of course, if they had paced themselves more carefully and not over-exerted, they could have kept on pedaling as long as I did. I was also cheered by the thought that if I forced myself to keep spinning with Melissa, I would learn more self-control at the dining room table. No cake had been invented yet that was worth this kind of punishment, though a double fudge torte came close.

As the class eventually ground to its merciful conclusion, Melissa said, "Ladies and gentlemen, please do not dismount until your bikes have come to a complete stop. Remember that many body parts may have shifted during class, so be extremely careful during your dismount. We thank you for spinning with Buff Bodies, Inc., and hope that you will spin with us again soon."

At home, I walked in the door like a character in a spaghetti western, only without the ten-gallon hat. Of course, I must now purge the word "spaghetti" from my vocabulary, except in the case of the aforementioned type of movie or as an adjective describing a kind of shoulder strap that I am unsuited to wear.

Today I am walking even funnier than I did yesterday, and many body parts are beginning to ache. I'm satisfied that yesterday's exertions were so successful, but I'm afraid it's going to be a long winter.

I Have My Head Examined, and Regret It

From the time the earliest cavemen and cavewomen scraped their knuckles across the savannah, people have suffered from headaches. Even way back then, many of these afflictions were induced by job stress. After all, cave people lacked many of the modern amenities that make careers today so rewarding, such as Internet gambling and company-mandated diversity training. Other headaches may have been caused by the sneaking suspicion that indoor plumbing was still 6,000 years away.

As a longtime headache sufferer, I am profoundly grateful that medical science has evolved from the days when headaches were cured by drilling a large hole in the skull to ward off evil spirits or demons. It may have been extreme, but this technique had its own weird genius. At least you could be sure that after the cave doctor aimed his sterilized spear at your cranium, you would never have another headache as long as you lived, which was probably about seven seconds.

It didn't take long for clever Cro-Magnon physicians to perceive that this approach to pain management put a serious crimp on their monthly billables, so they began to devise other headache treatments, such as Lydia Pinkham's Vegetable Compound. Yet headaches continued to plague mankind. And they seemed to really have it out for womankind, who have popularized the line "Not tonight dear, I have a headache," because they out-headache men by a margin of nearly two to one.

I have had headaches—and their big, bad, brother, migraines—since the Reagan administration. (Some of them even seem to last as long as the Reagan administration did.) Lately, they have gotten a lot worse, so I decided to go to the doctor.

"What brings you here today?" the doctor asked.

"Migraines," I answered.

"How long have you had them?" The doctor held her pen aloft, poised to write my answer.

"Since the Reagan administration," I answered.

She stared at me in disbelief. "That long?" she asked.

"I was waiting for my HMO to approve the office visit," I explained.

I asked my doctor to order many expensive tests to help explain my noggin-banging, vision-blurring, nausea-inducing plague. Even if the tests were worthless, at least I'd feel that I was starting to get my money's worth out of our crippling monthly health insurance payments. They don't call them "premiums" for nothing.

My doctor obliged me by sending me off for an MRI, which made me feel important. The MRI was a huge machine that would suck me into its narrow tunnel to take photos of my head. The test results would determine whether I was doomed to live with migraines for no reason, or whether I was just plain doomed.

I lay down on the table, and noticed with some anxiety that my young technician wore a sweatshirt emblazoned with "Nightmare on Elm Street" on the front, surrounded by a medley of ghoulish skulls.

"You're not claustrophobic, are you?" she asked.

"Who me? Of course not," I said as she pressed a button

that zipped me deep into the bowels of the machine, where I discovered to my surprise that I was in fact absolutely, clinically, and irredeemably claustrophobic. I felt like I could barely breathe. There wasn't even enough room for oxygen molecules.

"You okay in there?"

"No!"

"Great!" she said. "Get ready for the first photo. It'll last about forty-five seconds and it may be a smidgen loud."

"Help!" I said from the depths, forcing myself to take deep, slow breaths to avoid a total freak-out. The woman instructed me to lie still (as if I even had room to blink) and close my eyes. The "smidgen loud" noises were jackhammer blasts in my ears. Over the next half-hour, my Nightmare on Elm Street technician warned me about each upcoming photo and the "slightly loud" noises I might notice. I had always thought of photography as a quiet process (except for when people all shout "cheese!"), but these photos sounded like car alarms and jam sessions with Metallica and Iron Maiden, each vying to see who could snap one another's eardrums the fastest.

Although I hadn't had a migraine when I arrived, the heavy metal symphony in my ears ensured that I left with a whopper. For several days afterward, I waited anxiously for the results. Finally, the doctor called.

"Your MRI is fine," she said.

"Are you sure?" I asked. I was planning how to divvy up my good jewelry among relatives. "Then what else do you recommend?" I asked.

"Try to avoid stress. Also, try eliminating caffeine, wheat, cheese, MSG, nitrates, and chocolate from your diet. Then call me in two weeks."

Eliminate stress? Stop eating MSG and chocolate, two of

my favorite food groups? The very idea was blasphemous. If I had to live like this, I would become the poster child for the National Headache Foundation.

My migraines have decreased since my MRI, and I attribute this felicitous trend to a surge in my consumption of MSG and chocolate. Just don't tell my doctor.

Walk a Mile with My Pedometer

It does not augur well when you must suck in your gut and hold your breath as if you are having multiple X-rays taken simply to zip up your skirt.

When this happened to me, I knew I had two choices: Give up my current wardrobe or lose the excess baggage. Since I had recently written a book on diet and exercise that ended with my buying a new, smaller wardrobe, I decided it would be too embarrassing to blow up like a float in the Macy's Thanksgiving Day parade. Better that I should return to vigorous exercise and horrid Weight Watcher bars.

I perused several fitness magazines I had at home and found an article about walking. "Brisk walking is one of the best forms of cardiovascular exercise, even for out-of-shape marshmallows like you," the article explained. "It is suitable for all ages and abilities and requires no special equipment beyond a good pair of walking shoes and a commitment not to double-dip into the cookie jar. A simple, affordable pedometer or step counter can help motivate you to a more active lifestyle."

Eureka! I live in a large city where I could walk to many stores and businesses, so this plan could work for me. I jumped in the car and drove to the nearest sporting goods store to buy my pedometer. Why walk there before I knew how many calories I'd be burning in the process? Besides, no sense knocking myself out so early in the day, leaving no energy for a brisk walk later on.

I chose a fitness pedometer that would track my mileage, steps taken, and calories burned. I declined the pedometer that barked out peppy rah-rah encouragement, such as "You're doing great!" How would a pedometer know if I were struggling up a hill or just walking to the freezer to get a bowl of Haagen-Dazs? The article also noted that in today's lazy society, most people walk a measly 2,000 steps on a typical day. My goal should be at least 6,000 steps, but if I wanted to see real results I had better ramp it up to 10,000.

Not surprisingly, I had trouble figuring out how to operate the device, but after an hour and a half on the phone with a patient customer service representative, I was programmed for fitness!

Ready for action, I clipped the pedometer to my skirt and strode energetically to the front door to see if the mail had come. I took twenty-three steps and burned three calories. Then I took the dog around the block—198 steps taken and nine more calories gone. Borrowing a cup of flour from a friend around the corner tallied another seventy-nine steps and eleven calories. I could see that it was going to be a long way to 10,000 steps.

I refused to let my enthusiasm flag, even as I wondered how to meet my daily walking quota while also completing my regular work. Most of my "must-do" work involves sitting at a computer or tending pots on a stove. I planned to squeeze in as many steps as possible by following other advice from the article: parking my car in a shopping center a half-mile from the one where I intended to shop; taking the stairs, even if I had an appointment on the twenty-third floor; going for a lunch hour stroll (the writer made no mention of when I might actually get to eat lunch); and my favorite: marching in place while I'm on the phone.

Then I hustled over to the mall for some new walking shoes, which would prove essential to keep my spirits up. I parked in a far corner on the uppermost level of the parking structure where I had never parked before. I assumed, correctly as it turned out, that I would not be able to locate my car afterwards and therefore would log at least another half-mile in aimless wandering.

At the mall, I tried to remember all the article's walking posture instructions: I kept my head up and centered between my shoulders (where else would I keep my head?), my eyes focused straight ahead (as opposed to having my eyes darting like a psychotic?), my chest lifted, swinging my arms and hands at a ninety-degree angle (too bad; I much prefer an eighty-five-degree angle). I had no idea how to do all this while also pulling my belly button in toward my spine and tucking my pelvis forward so that I could feel taller than my paltry five feet, three inches. One wonders how our ancestors managed to walk throughout history without expert advice on how to put one foot in front of the other.

I lost my train of thought when I spotted a strange character striding confidently toward the food court. I couldn't tell if it was male or female, but it was wearing woman's clothing. I picked up the pace and followed the mystery shopper, but it was fast! Out of breath, I finally got close enough to see that he was a transvestite, carrying a very trendy purse in aubergine. I was tempted to go up and ask him where he got that purse, but I couldn't afford to get sidetracked from my mission. I checked my pedometer. Stalking the transvestite burned another twenty-one calories.

My foray to the mall yielded an impressive 987 steps, 503 of which were spent finding the car. Despite this exertion, my pedometer only claimed a sixty-two-calorie burn.

Donning my new athletic shoes, I took the dog for a mega-calorie burning walk. Fitness walking with a dog is a unique form of "interval training." When Ken sees a squirrel or other enticing creature, he runs like a rocket, forcing me to hurtle after him. But his insistence on stopping to sniff every other tree gives my heart a chance to recover from the last squirrel sighting. We returned home and I eagerly checked the pedometer. I had gone 2.5 miles, including hills, but only burned 198 calories! How could this be? My walking article claimed that a vigorous forty-five-minute walk should burn up to 350 calories!

I realized the pedometer was faulty, and I called the manufacturer to complain.

"There's something wrong with. . . your. . . pedometers," I huffed. "It's. . . not. . . (huff huff) showing that. . . I. . . burned. . . enough calories."

"There's nothing wrong with our pedometers," a surly female agent told me. "Besides, if you're that out of breath from making a phone call, it's no wonder you can't walk very far."

"I'm out of . . . breath because. . . I'm jumping up and down to burn. . . more calories! That's what the. . . article on. . . walking for. . . fitness told (huff huff) me to do!"

"Maybe you didn't program your pedometer correctly," she asked. "Is your weight correct?"

"No, my weight is not correct!" I had stopped jumping at this point, worried that I might trip an unfortunate cardiac emergency. "It is unjust in the extreme. That's why I bought this blasted pedometer in the first place!" I realized that I was not advancing my cause by having an emotional breakdown while on the phone with this unsympathetic person. How could she possibly understand? I bet she had only twelve percent body fat.

I got no relief from my conversation, but I persevered. Five days later I had walked 19.7 miles, or 43,637 steps, burning 1,616 calories. This included walking to the bakery, where I slaked my sorrow in a large cinnamon bun and coffee. Despite this, today I did not have to hold my breath until I nearly turned blue to zip my skirt. It was a subtle difference, but a difference nonetheless. Progress was coming, one electronically measured step at a time. But I'm not kidding myself: I've miles to go before I'm sleek.

The Purpose-Driven Illness

A great Yiddish expression says, "It's better to be able to say, 'I used to be sick' than 'I used to be rich.'" I have never been rich, but like most of us, I have been sick—in fact, being sick was my sorry condition all last week.

Few people would guess that there is a right way and a wrong way to be sick. Sure, some family members claimed that I made it look easy, but in reality, it has taken years of conscientious practice to elevate the state of sickliness into an art form. So now, just in time for flu season, I humbly offer my personal recommendations on How to Be Sick.

How to Be Sick

1. When you are too sickly even to watch Comedy Central, count the stretch marks on your abdomen that you collected during your pregnancies. Use a calculator if necessary. For added impact, begin this examination around the time you expect the kids to arrive home from school. No need to lock your bedroom door. The kids would never think to come and see how you are, when they have a roller coaster theme park to build on the computer. You'll know they're home when you hear the thunk of backpacks dropping like cluster bombs in the living room and smell burnt microwave popcorn wafting down the hall, making you feel nauseated.

2. Walk unsteadily to the bathroom, take out your magnifying mirror, and look for signs of aging. Pretend your head contains

one of those computers that can redraw faces to look ten, twenty, and thirty years older than you are now. Focus on how you might appear twenty years from now, and don't forget to imagine thinning hair, too. Return to bed.

3. To generate more sympathy for your condition, call a friend when your voice is so weak you can barely be heard. Listen as your friend instantly launches into a tale of her own symptoms, including stomach nausea and weight loss of five pounds. Be cagey when she asks how much weight you have lost, answering only that you heard it's dangerous to get on an electronic scale when you have a fever of more than 104.

4. Using your trusty hand mirror again, practice looking haggard and miserable for the moment when your kids do enter your room to issue a variety of demands. These will include: When are you going to get up and type my English essay? Didn't you remember that it's due tomorrow? When are you going to the store, since we are out of jelly and Eggo waffles? When are we going to the pet store to get a new hamster, because you promised! (The hamster, now of blessed memory, died right before you spiked a fever. The wheel in his empty cage now stands as a silent accuser to your apparent preference to staying in bed and trying to calm your involuntary bodily chills rather than keep a promise to a young child. And you have the temerity to call yourself a mother!)

5. Examine the holiday gift catalogs that are arriving by the cartload each day and imagine how nice you would look in the sapphire earrings and matching necklace that are too preposterously expensive to expect anyone to ever buy for you. Feel sorry for yourself.

6. Allow the dog to spend his day with you, shedding all over your pajamas as he curls up next to your febrile body. Don't bother trying to kick him out when he growls or barks, which will be approximately every four minutes. He'll only come back.

7. Listen to news reports about the flu outbreak and the national shortage of flu vaccine. Pay special attention to updated reports of hospitalizations due to complications of flu. Then try to relax and take a nap, if you can manage to move the dog, who is snoring.

8. To help you sleep, take both a sleep aid *and* some of your husband's Sudafed before bed. Then, as you wonder why you are unable to fall asleep, remember that although the Sudafed was marked as a "non-drowsy" formulation, this was really code for "will make you incredibly hyper for at least twelve hours." Gnash your teeth in frustration until dawn, when you fall asleep for a short time until the dog licks your face—his signal that he needs to be let out.

9. Turn on the television, and shudder in fear for the fate of our culture. Turn off the television.

10. Read something uplifting, such as "The U.S. Armed Forces Nuclear, Biological and Chemical Survival Manual."

11. Finally, examine your life, your ambitions, your dreams, and consider how far short you are from having achieved any of these laughable goals. Make a list of new, more reasonable goals to help you with personal growth while limiting your potential for failure. Begin the list with a plan to throw out the remaining Sudafed.

12. You can well imagine that following my simple principles for How to Be Sick will give you just the motivation you need to get well as quickly as possible. And when that happy day comes, you will bound out of bed with zealous gratitude for your health and well-being. Not only that, you can finally put away the vaporizer. In the meantime, drink plenty of liquids, take two vitamins with dinner, and just try to relax.

EuroChump

While I was hard at work making my face fit to be seen at a swanky restaurant, my husband became impatient. I don't know why. I had been in the bathroom only for an hour and a half. When he reminded me that we were in danger of losing our restaurant reservation, I cracked open the bathroom door and assured him that I'd only need another ten minutes. Fifteen, max.

"What's all this stuff on the counter?" he asked, surveying the gaggle of jars, vials, squeeze tubes and bottles. Frankly, it looked like a science experiment gone wrong.

"It's my new skin care line, and each product must be applied in exactly the right order for best results," I said. "They say that if I faithfully apply every potion every day for at least six months, results will be immediate."

Within twenty minutes, my face lay hidden under more layers than King Tut. I don't know if the concoctions had really erased any fine lines and signs of aging, but someone would have had to sandblast through all the levels of emollients on my kisser to find them. Following the instructions in the brochure, I had focused like a cosmetic surgeon's laser beam on which creams to dab, which to gently apply in clockwise circles (never counter-clockwise!), which to spray and then let dry for exactly four minutes, and which to pat all over, not neglecting the neck area. Since these laboratory masterpieces were sumptuously priced, I gasped in horror after accidentally shooting a wad of the Anti-Wrinkle, Anti-Gravity Rejuvenating Night Reform Alpha Lipoic Serum in the sink instead of on my hand. That mistake alone must have cost me five bucks.

How did I get suckered into this in the first place? To deflect any personal responsibility, I'm blaming it all on my neighbor, Joline. I happened to walk by her house the day she launched her distributorship of EuroChump, the "revolutionary" new patented skin care system. I tried to hurry past her house, but I was spotted while she was tying balloons on her front porch, and she insisted I come in for some samples.

Two hours later, in a fog, I, too, was a EuroChump distributor. Like someone snatched into a Scientology temple, I was forced to study the EuroChump catechism in Joline's living room. In alarmingly short order, I soon became convinced that only an imbecile would ever apply a finishing moisturizer containing almond extract before applying the anti-gravity environmental shield recovery serum. These products were to women's skin care what the Pentagon's missile defense shield was to national security, namely, costly and unproven buffers against enemy incursions.

I felt a sinking sense of peril immediately after entering Joline's house, and silently repeated the mantra, "Don't buy! Don't buy!" I closed my eyes and conjured visions of my most recent bank statement, revealing punishing overdraft charges. But Joline swore on her great-uncle Silvio's grave that EuroChump would combat signs of aging, rejuvenate my skin, render Botox treatments a thing of the past, and lower my cholesterol. I thought of the substantial inventory of other skin care wares fossilizing in my medicine cabinet. They, too, had all promised the fountain of eternal skin youth. But a look in the mirror proved that their dealers were simply cads and liars. I was still older! And I still looked it!

Under these cruel circumstances, could it hurt just to look at what EuroChump had to offer? I reached out for a tester tube of an inviting-looking cream, but Joline swatted away my hand.

"Our anti-aging products are over *here*," she instructed me, determined not to sell me anything designed for women who might still get carded when buying liquor.

I tried not to take it personally that the names of each anti-aging product in the EuroChump line began with the letters "Re," a prefix that essentially means, "Do over." These included a "Reconstruction" *gelée*, as if my face had survived the Battle of Gettysburg. Other products "renewed," "recovered," "repaired," "reactivated," "rejuvenated," "reformed," and "restored." This didn't sound like a beauty line; it sounded like a public works project.

Of course, this wasn't all. For more serious cases of dermatological neglect, EuroChump hustled another line called "Repent," which, if you bought the entire set of eighteen products, would probably require you to "Refinance." Naturally (since all EuroChump products were completely natural), these offerings were *gelée* not gels, and *crèmes*, not creams, because EuroChump was whipped up in some lab in Switzerland, a quirky kind of nation that excels only in the creation of skin care products, timepieces (the better to gauge how fast your skin is aging), chocolate (the better to make your face break out, requiring more skin care potions), and secret bank accounts (the better to hide all the vats of currency rolling into the coffers of companies such as EuroChump). I never understood why skin care and make-up that sounds French has always had so much *cachet*. After all, can't America also produce exotic ingredients such as cucumber fruit extract and cellulose gum?

Since I had downloaded so many dollars to upgrade my dermis, I was almost dutiful in following EuroChump's day care and night care routines. I hoped that my face could tell time, since it needed to respond differently to the night *crème* applied at 11:00 p.m. versus how it was to behave upon receiving the day moisturizer at 7:00 a.m. But it must have, since a few people began to compliment me on my face.

"You're looking radiant today," a friend remarked. Did she sound envious? I could only hope. My hairdresser, who is hard to please in this area, deigned to call my complexion "absolutely dewy." Well, I thought, it was about time that someone noticed my reconstructed, rejuvenated, repaired, re-hydrated and refinanced skin!

So far, I cannot regret my indulgence of the EuroChump line, but I have a new problem: Now that I've got the skin care basics down, I'm going to have to upgrade all my old fossilizing make-up, too.

The Perfect Woman: What's She Hiding?

Have you ever had the misfortune to meet the "perfect" woman? I mean the one who is at the gym at six in the morning, has her kids at school in the dent-free minivan by eight, and is at the office by nine, where she leads her department in sales, not only for the last fiscal quarter, but for the entire *year?* Worse, she also has the audacity to be slender and well-dressed. She doesn't look a day older now than she did fifteen years ago.

Part of you—the part that wants to watch reality television instead of doing something productive—wants to hate her, because topping it all off, she is also a gourmet cook. Last time you spoke to her, she casually mentioned plans to finally write that cookbook just so she doesn't have to keep giving out the same recipes over and over to all the people who call for them. Naturally, any proceeds from book sales will go to cancer research. Oh, and did I mention that she ran the Marathon?

But because she is so nice, you cannot hate her. You cannot hate a woman who showed up at your doorstep with hot lasagna that she made for your family when you were in bed with the flu. (Thankfully, someone else greeted her at the door, sparing you the sight of her in a chic silk pantsuit and high-heeled sling backs.) You cannot despise a woman kind enough to have taken your kids for the weekend so that you and your husband could go away, and then—when the kids were discovered to be lice-infested—began to de-louse them herself. You didn't even discover their horrid condition until you came home. No, it would take a blackguard to loathe a woman this perfect, yet so very, very *nice*. The best you might content yourself with is to imagine that she is hiding something dark and terrible, such as unsightly varicose veins, or kleptomania.

How can we mere mortal women learn to cope with the existence of these paragons of energy, virtue, talent and—perhaps most unforgivable—weight control? How can we protect ourselves from feeling like slackers if we bought our kid's birthday cake from Costco while we know that *she* stayed up till two in the morning baking a cake that looked like a pirate ship? How can we preserve our self-esteem when we are working beneath our creative abilities just to pay the bills and still bringing in take-out a few nights a week while she is rising like a rocket to upper management in the field of her dreams?

The bottom line is, sisterhood may be powerful, but comparisons are poison. I learned long ago that it was useless to compare myself to Lonny, who is so organized that even with five kids she has never lost a library book. Or to Cassie, who works full time but also logs many hours a month volunteering at a soup kitchen. Or to Mary, who despite long years of singledom and a gallery of regrettable dates has never lost her smile or her grace.

Sometimes, faced with yet another woman of stellar accomplishments, I fretted: *What am I, chopped liver?* I sure felt like it, but since it is not my habit to drown my sorrows in chopped liver, I ate chocolate chip cookies in despair. Clearly, this was not a winning plan.

Fortunately, I came up with a better plan. This plan was to learn to celebrate the sisterhood as a whole, and to refrain from imagining varicose veins or a prior criminal record on one of the overly accomplished women around me (Even the gourmet cook who is also a rocket scientist). I learned it was okay for me to just say no if the hospitality committee of my synagogue asked me to make a meal for a family during a week where my energy was maxed out like a credit card. And I accepted the fact that even if Lonnie never, ever amasses a library fine exceeding fifty cents in her whole life, I will continue to lose books and pay fines. (However, at least this makes me a *true* patron of the library.)

Groucho Marx famously said, "I wouldn't want to belong to any club that would accept me as a member." Hey, I'm lucky to belong to a group of amazing women orbiting my universe who *do* accept me as a member. So, even if I never manage to get to the gym each morning at six, or serve three different appetizers from recipes in *Bon Appetit,* or even though for sure I'll never be a rocket scientist, at least I'm a part of their club. And that's a good place to be.

And That's a Wrap

Today I visited heaven for nearly three hours. It's a really nice place, and I highly recommend it.

One of the best things about heaven is that it's a cell phone and pager-free zone. People speak in hushed tones, and then only to ask solicitous questions such as, "May I refill your glass of lemon water?" or "May I take you now for your organic enzyme facial?" If this isn't heaven, I don't know what is.

It's always casual Friday in heaven. Everyone wears long terry robes made of Egyptian cotton, though they are mighty heavy for such a lofty atmosphere. We pad gently down the marble hallways in our rubber flip-flops as we grapple with the only decisions required of us: Should we repose in a La-Z-Boy recliner and dip our hands and feet in essential oils before having our nails painted? Or should we loll around in the Misting Room, where a cool aromatic mist sprays us from the ceiling, refreshing us after an exhausting session in the Jacuzzi?

Maids discreetly offer warm towels, plates of sliced apples, and pretend not to see your cellulite when you change into your bathing suit for a dunk in the whirlpool.

My husband sent me to The Indulgence Inn for my birthday. He's a smart man, and is now assured several more years of marital happiness.

I waited to be summoned for my Calming Detox Wrap

("wakes up your senses and sets your body tingling!") in the "Quiet Room," where silence is appreciated. I hoped I wasn't making too much noise by turning the pages of *Golf Digest* or by my steady, even breathing. My only serious gripe with The Indulgence Inn was its surprisingly limp magazine selection. How many issues of aged *People* magazines can anyone take in a single afternoon?

My "wrapper," Angela, efficiently mummified me in forty hot Irish linen sheets, which had been drenched in a concoction of Chinese herbs. She sealed up the sheet package with some kind of wax paper, followed by a layer of heavy-duty aluminum foil, the kind I would use for a big roast. When she was done, I lurked far beneath the surface, looking like something that belonged on a NASA shuttle. Soft sitar music wafted in, and I was too blissed-out to care whether these herb-soaked sheets would chase toxins out of my system or not. Although Angela wraps people in aluminum foil for a living, she is called a "therapist" at the Inn. In fact, everyone is a therapist there, including the cashier. This makes sense, as one just might need psychological succor when realizing how much it costs to bankroll a few hours of relaxation.

One thing I noticed at the Inn was that the ickier the materials involved in a treatment, the more it cost. For example, my herbal wrap was less expensive than the thermal seaweed wrap. But who in their right mind wants to pay a hundred and fifty bucks to be wrapped in seaweed? Similarly, a mud bath ("every pore will sigh with relief") is pricier than a wrap in eucalyptus leaves. If I had known that I could have charged eighty-five bucks to slather people in mud, I would never have paved over the backyard.

After my Swedish massage, I could hardly put one wobbly foot in front of the other. Frankly, if I had been any more relaxed I would have been comatose. Back in the Quiet Room, I waited to be called for my facial, an ordeal that involved much rubbing and stretching of skin. During my facial, I had an epiphany: This was the first time I ever had a facial steam treatment other than when I opened the dishwasher in the middle of a load. I had also looked forward to having cucumbers placed over my eyelids, like they show in the magazines, but my facial therapist, Lisa, only slapped a pair of goggles on my eyes as she cast a harsh light on my face.

"You have very clean pores," she declared, while spraying my face with something lemony, yet with a hint of rosemary. It smelled like something that would go well on salmon.

"Why thank you, I murmured. "I take my pore health very seriously."

After Lisa proclaimed my face fully exfoliated, extracted, cleansed, steamed, and hydrated, I begged to stay and take a nap, but she hauled me off the table to make room for the next client.

Reluctantly, I prepared to leave heaven. I took a last, lingering look at the Jacuzzi and watched as the ubiquitous maids continued to proffer fruits and lemon water all around. As I turned in my locker key at the front desk, an unnerving thought intruded on my mind: When I got home, I had to make dinner.

On a more cheery note, I thought, my next birthday is now only 364 days away.

A Crime of Passion,
Featuring Chocolate Truffles

For six weeks I had been tormented by close contact with a box of truffles, yet until last week I had not touched a single one.

This would not be noteworthy if I were speaking of the kind of truffle that is an expensive fungus and which is odious even to contemplate. No, I'm talking Godiva dark chocolate truffles, the kind that will induce swooning in any self-respecting chocoholic. If I may brag, I believe this degree of self-restraint was remarkable on my part. Yet who among us doesn't have a breaking point?

Just for the record, Godiva chocolates are not a staple on my regular shopping list. Laundry detergent, Milk Bones for the dog, low-fat cottage cheese, yes. Even Splenda-infused, sugar-free chocolate ribbon "ice cream" gets tossed in the cart. But Godiva chocolates? *Au contraire!*

I had bought the truffles as a special indulgence for my husband on his birthday. Those of you already suspicious of my true motives for this purchase are correct: I was banking on him sharing the stash. In my defense, buying the Godivas had been an act of desperation. As my husband's birthday loomed closer, I was flummoxed about choosing a gift. Like a lot of men, he's hard to buy for. He doesn't hunt, fish, or whittle wood into ducks in the garage. I even toyed with the notion of buying him a new four-iron club until I remembered that he doesn't golf, either. He has enough ties to outfit all of Wall Street. He is maddeningly un-materialistic.

I try not to hold this against him. But as a considerate wife, I strive to make gift buying for my birthday as easy as possible. Over the years, I have let him know—with the gentlest of hints—that I can be happy with a vast variety of things. Diamonds, sapphires, Caribbean cruises, all are fine with me. After all, I hate to be a burden.

As his birthday approached, I finally ordered tickets to a concert, but that event was several weeks off. I still needed a little something for him on his special day. Passing by a Godiva store in the mall, I felt the spirit move me, not to mention a timely rumbling in my tummy.

Unfortunately, my spouse has an odd personality quirk. He's neither a "foodie" nor a chocoholic. To him, eating is just a pesky nuisance interrupting an otherwise productive workday. Given the huge chasm between our approaches to food, it is amazing that our marriage has proved so durable. It didn't surprise me that days and weeks after his birthday, he seemed to forget that he was only an arm's length from these delectable truffles, not to mention the opportunity to share them with me. As a result, each day he went off to work and the kids went to school, leaving me alone in the house with the Godivas. Alone. Unsupervised. And yearning.

I tried to put it out of my mind, but the thought of those truffles sitting in the refrigerator harassed me. I tinkered with the fridge's thermostat to make sure I wasn't over-chilling the delicacies. Their ultimate purpose in life was to be eaten, preferably by a card-carrying chocoholic like me. How long would they have to wait to fulfill their cocoa-dusted destiny? My husband would not have said anything had I dipped into a French vanilla truffle, but deep down, would he think less of me if I proved to be a woman of easy chocolate virtue?

I wrestled with my conscience. If pressed, I could justify consuming my husband's birthday truffles on health grounds. Research has proven time and time again that the antioxidants in dark chocolate enhance the functioning of important cells in blood vessels. Volunteers in one study who ate 100 grams of dark chocolate experienced improved endothelial functioning lasting for at least three hours. I'm not sure what endothelial functioning means, but it sounds critically important. With the Godivas in the house, I could keep my endothelials functioning like a well-oiled machine just by eating dark chocolate every three hours!

On the other hand, a theft is a theft. Besides, I live with enough regrets, such as the time last week when I stood in the ten-items or less line in the supermarket when I knew darned well I had thirteen items. And, while I'm confessing here, I once shorted the newspaper delivery boy a Christmas bonus, and don't think he ever let me live that down. For six months afterward, he tossed our paper in the neighbor's thorny bushes, and I still have the scrapes to prove it. Would I now compound these moral lapses by buckling under the pressure of a mochacinno chocolate truffle with an espresso-flavored mousse and vanilla-cream center?

It became harder to remain absorbed in the serious business of writing humor each day while the thought of those truffles gnawed at me. I felt my resolve crumbling like so many stale Oreos. It was time for decisive action.

That night after dinner, I waved the box—still with its plastic wrapping and chocolate brown ribbon—in front of my husband and demanded that he eat at least one. "Maybe later," he said as he headed out the door. "I'm going to clear the rain gutters now. They're predicting rain." I felt a chocolate meltdown coming on.

There was an easy, obvious solution to the problem. I could leave the box on the table, call the kids, and the truffles would be history. But I couldn't bring myself to allow children who think that Nestlé's milk chocolate is a delicacy to tear into a box of Godiva truffles.

After my husband had cleared the rain gutters, I stalked him around the house with the chocolates. "If you care about my mental health and my waistline you will begin to eat your birthday chocolates—*now*," I demanded. This got his attention. Taking the box from me, he noticed the price, which I had forgotten to remove. "You paid this much for eight chocolates?"

"No price is too high to celebrate a man of your caliber," I said, wanting him to get on with it. I believe that knowing how much I paid for the truffles may have soured his appetite, but he dutifully ate the smooth coconut truffle. In the spirit of togetherness, I had the double chocolate raspberry.

That was two weeks ago and he hasn't taken a single other truffle since. This morning I decided I could no longer take responsibility for his continued shilly-shallying over the Godivas. Boldly, I opened the box to enjoy a piece with a mid-morning cup of coffee, and was shocked to discover that two more truffles were missing! Obviously, one of the children found my secret hiding place for the truffles, behind the pre-washed arugula. (I really didn't imagine anyone would check there.) It's only a matter of time before this same thief absconds with the rest. No wonder that society worries about the declining moral standards of today's youth.

Not wanting to become an accessory to a crime committed by minors, I ate a French vanilla truffle. And then a dark chocolate one.

Now there are only three left. If I can force my husband to have another one after dinner tonight, I should have this box finished by Wednesday, and this entire sorry episode of the truffles will be behind me—literally.

Next year, when my husband's birthday rolls around, he just may find himself with that four-iron after all.

Haunted by the Ghost of Doctor Atkins

Over the past few months, I have relished the apparent collapse of the low-carb industry. Low-carb specialty stores and magazines arrived with much fanfare but soon crumbled like a tired soufflé. Good riddance to them, I thought (especially the low-carb magazine that bilked me after I wrote an article for them). Low-carbism was just another sorry scheme to part consumers from their hard-earned bucks and their bagels. And who could afford the stuff? I tried an insanely expensive low-carb pasta once. It was heavy, gummy, and tasteless, and those were its finer qualities.

I realized my satisfaction was premature when I was confronted with a ghostly protégée of Dr. Atkins. She was draped in a size zero dress and toting a sorry slice of flourless bread between scrawny fingers. If she got any skinnier her DNA would show.

The timing couldn't have been worse. I was happily toting a batch of homemade bread and a broccoli quiche to a potluck birthday party, eager for some good fun and good eats. But I had barely crossed the threshold when Sandy, the hostess and erstwhile birthday girl, announced that she had lost another ten pounds on the Atkins plan. Sandy had always been as slim as an asparagus spear. Why she felt compelled to whittle down as thin as a blade of wheat grass was beyond me. And telling me bordered on the cruel. I forced a smile at her "achievement" as I placed my culinary contributions on the table.

"Mmmm, smells good," Sandy said, leaning over to inhale the bread. If she were still Atkinizing herself, could I blame her for wanting a little inhalation therapy of a wheat product? "This is home-baked, isn't it?" I detected a plaintive quality to her question.

"Yes, and I made the broccoli quiche, too."

"Is it crustless?" Hope returned to her voice.

"Uh, no, I'm sorry. I didn't realizing you were still no-carbing it."

"I'm not no-carbing it, I'm *low*-carbing it," she clarified.

"But Sandy, it's your birthday, for crying out loud. Can't you allow yourself a measly fifty or sixty carbs today? I mean, look at you! When you turn sideways you disappear!"

Sandy was saved from answering by a knock at the door. Linda and Rachel had arrived, the heavenly aroma of something Italian wafting in after them.

Soon, all the guests had settled around the table. I sliced my bread and passed the basket around. Sandy immediately passed the basket to Linda. Meanwhile, I saw her stealthily remove from under her napkin a very dark, very thin slice of bread filled with sprouty-looking things.

"What *is* that?" Linda asked. It appeared to have been made from at least forty percent recycled paper products.

"It's flourless protein bread," Sandy explained. It was called Ezekiel 4.9, "as described in the holy Bible," according to the package, made from lentils, barley, and spelt, whatever that was. Just what we all needed: a "friend" seemingly bent on becoming skinnier than Lindsay Lohan, and a loaf of bread that quoted scripture. Sandy offered us all a piece, and we each took polite little bites.

"Who says there's no truth in advertising?" I asked. "This actually tastes biblical!"

"I thought the Atkins thing was over," Linda chimed in helpfully, washing down her Ezekiel 4.9 with an eight-ounce cup of H_2O.

"Not for me," Sandy said. "I'm almost at my high school cheerleading weight, which is my goal. You may think it's silly," she admitted, ejecting a carrot curl from her salad as if it carried the avian flu.

Rachel was busily serving up a nice portion of the broccoli quiche and some low-fat manicotti. She said, "My sister-in-law is going one better than you, Sandy. She's only eating raw foods."

"That sounds exhausting," I said. "Who has that much time to chew?"

"She says it makes her feel light," Rachel answered.

"If I want to feel that light, I'll float in the Dead Sea," I said. Was I sounding a tad snarky? I couldn't help it. I had been looking forward to this birthday party and the guest of honor was ruining it for me. If only Sandy had warned us all in advance, we could have saved ourselves a lot of trouble and prepared a meal that she could have eaten without picking out half the ingredients, such as a plate of cheese slices and broiled zucchini. Rachel had made her famous Big Fat Greek Salad, but I was distracted by the sight of Sandy making a little hill of the croutons and shunting aside all the tomatoes as well. What a waste of all that vitamin C!

I didn't say so at the time, but it didn't seem to me that Dr. Atkins' dietary brainstorm helped him very much, either. After all, he died after taking a fall. Seems to me if he'd had a little more padding on him, he probably could have just gotten up, dusted himself off, and gone on his merry way. Of course, the Atkins people like to keep this quiet, but I also heard his cholesterol was higher than the

Dow Jones Industrial Average. Despite all his efforts, you still never hear anybody say, "That's the greatest thing since sliced celery!"

Inevitably, dessert time arrived. We all sang happy birthday to Sandy, but I wasn't feeling so happy anymore. The unspoken pressure during lunch had made me peel off the pasta from the manicotti, and even I was reduced to foregoing the croutons on the Greek salad. It's amazing how fast mass hysteria can spread.

Rachel served her luscious carrot cake, and Sandy blew out the candles before eating one of them. But no matter how long she sat there, no way could Sandy pick out all the microscopic pieces of carrot from a slab of carrot cake. However, it all worked out in the end. While the rest of us ate the actual cake, we scraped off the cream cheese frosting and gave it to Sandy.

The Bikini: A Risk to National Security

Before Congress breaks for their summer recess, I hope they'll carve out a little time to outlaw the bikini. There are three reasons for this that should be obvious to everyone.

First, the bikini creates a hostile sunning environment for women. The sight of nubile young females in public wearing only enough material to equal four paper clips prompts a surge in heart palpitations among normal-sized women. Women with stretch marks (who number approximately three billion, according to the World Health Organization) also suffer skyrocketing stress hormones in the bloodstream, as well as the phenomenon known as "sand rage." Clearly, this form of swimwear poses an unacceptable health risk to nearly all women.

Second, the sight of sinewy girls frolicking in near nakedness on the beach only encourages would-be illegal immigrants to try to storm the borders. Therefore, this is also an issue of national security.

Finally, bikini-wearing in full view of men increases global warming. In my proposed legislation, bikini-wearing would be a misdemeanor, but romping in a string bikini would be a felony. I know the legislation may not be popular, and I am not counting on Ted Kennedy's vote.

I'm not sure why women's swimwear has been eroding faster than the ozone layer. Experts predict that in only two years, bikinis would be discernible only through a microscope. (Although this would surely be a boon to the microscope industry.) Under these circumstances, can you blame any woman for the terror that strikes her heart as summer begins?

Editors of women's magazines understand this, which is why they must lure their readers in by promising pages of "Stress-Free Swimwear!" Despite the upbeat headline, the small print reveals the truth: Picking a bathing suit is easy. . . for the "lucky few." These "lucky few" translate into only eight women in the known universe who can saunter into a dressing room, try on the skimpiest of bikinis, and emerge with her ego unshattered. The only hope for the rest of us 3.5 billion estrogen slaves is to invest in stylish beach cover-ups that will hide our Lycra-stuffed figures like cash in a dope dealer's suitcase.

Women wider than Nicole Kidman make huge sacrifices by accompanying our friends and family to the beach. But while the bikini-clad flirt with melanoma by reckless sun exposure, we wisely remain under wraps on a folding chair, massaging our brain cells with intellectual books on the Italian Renaissance. Okay, maybe we're reading the latest Janet Evanovich novel, but we would have read the book on the Italian Renaissance if the last copy hadn't been checked out at the library.

Meanwhile, normal women do have some options to survive swimsuit season without nervous breakdowns. First, stay away from the beach and the pools. Who needs them? The beaches are dirty, and God only knows what sludge will wash up on shore and weasel its way onto your person. As to pools, the chlorine gives everyone red eye, which is very unattractive.

However, you may not be able to slink out of beach or pool

visits. In extreme cases when you must be seen in a swimsuit, I recommend the following:

1. Knock back a couple of daiquiris before entering the dressing room with your swimsuits to dull the pain of your image under florescent lights. (This means you must take a designated non-swimsuit buyer with you to the mall.)

2. Avoid irresponsible and potentially lethal activities, such as trying on a swimsuit at Loehmann's. Who can ever forget the tragic results when a woman already teetering on the edge executed the infamous "Maillot Massacre" at a Loehmann's many years ago?

3. Stick with safe swimsuit bets, such as the "Hugger-Mugger," made from a specially patented material that promises to hide up to fifty pounds of French fries and ice cream sundaes in its snug shell. Frequent walking is recommended to avoid cutting off circulation.

4. Use the visual equivalent of pepper spray. The "Shrieking Silhouette," available in sizes up to 26W, is emblazoned with an optical print so garish it has caused blindness in scientific studies. Tummy overhangs up to the size of speed bumps and other "problem areas" are disguised under the dizzying graphics on the made-in-the-U.S.A Lycra. Anyone who looks directly at the suit will have instant vertigo, so they won't even notice the cellulite on your legs.

5. Summer in Saudi Arabia, where bikinis are a non-issue, except on pay-per-view television.

6. If all else fails, think side control panels, empire waists, and shelf bras (available at Home Depot).

Part IV:

Reading This Warning Label May Kill You (And Other Observations)

Who Needs Therapy Now?

For quite some time now my neighbor Molly has been in therapy to deal with her "issues." Since Molly doesn't drive, her live-in companion, Josie, takes her to the appointments. This is a rather extraordinary effort on Josie's part, since the therapist is located nearly 100 miles away.

Frankly, I haven't seen much change in Molly despite all the head-shrinking. She acts much like she always has: trotting along next to Josie, barking at suspicious-looking folks, and stopping to make wee-wee every fifth tree.

Molly is a thoroughly modern dog, with her therapy, haute doggity couture (including a fetching Saturday sailor suit and jaunty hat), and excursions to the mall. In fact, she lives a life similar to a lot of kids these days, only with less homework.

Not that long ago when gasoline was cheap and we drank water straight from the tap, dogs lived like, well, dogs. They had dog names, like Fido or Fetch, slept outside, ate dog food, chased squirrels, and generally were happy just to let their tongues hang out as much as possible.

All that has changed. Today's dogs expect a lot more out of life, and who can blame them? Dogs are the new kids, with names like Thurston or Brittany, designer wardrobes, and for some, regularly scheduled aromatherapy treatments and "furcials."

Dogs also have trumped kids as objects of admiration and

curiosity. For example, when I take a walk with one of my kids and our dog, passersby never fail to stop and say, "What a cute dog! How old is he? Is he a rescue? Where do you have him groomed?" Inquiring minds want to know all about Ken, but have zero curiosity about my kid. Don't they want to know if my kid was also a rescue? Have they no interest in where she gets her hair cut? Perhaps if I put a collar and a leash on my daughter people might notice her also. I would love to try this as an experiment, but my daughter has vetoed the idea.

I'm embarrassed about our dog's humanoid name, but it's not our fault. He was a rescue, in fact, and we were warned that we might inflict psychological damage by changing his name, given so many other stresses in his life at the time of the adoption. So he remained Ken and displayed psychological damage anyway by eating the living room couch for lunch every day and eating my sons' underwear for dessert. But with behavior this endearing, it was impossible to give him away.

Sure, we consider our dog a member of the family, sort of. Others believe the ties go even deeper. Crystal, who grooms him at Many Paws each month, always assures a nervous Ken, "Don't worry, baby, Mommy will come back for you soon." I never realized the resemblance between us was that striking.

Nearly all breeds are now easily confused with actual children, but based on my observations, Poodles, Pomeranians, Bichon Frises, and any "toy" breed top the faux-kid list. Last week, I waited in a pharmacy while a woman warned, "Mommy's leaving in three minutes, Sally!" to a six-pound ball of fur wearing slippers who had ambled behind the counter. Playing her role as mischievous child to the hilt, Sally refused to come out until Mommy played her trump card: "If you're not out by the count of three no treats from the Barkery today!" I stood riveted by the drama, unsure of the denouement, but when Sally heard the click-click of Mommy's heels on the floor she scrambled as fast as her four-inch high legs could carry her.

We once took Ken into the Barkery, just for laughs. It's like a Saks Fifth Avenue for dogs and cats, featuring cologne (tested on humans, not animals), jewelry, and clothing, including formal wear, biker chic, loungewear, and hats for every occasion: pink pillbox hats, cowboy hats and crushable, packable sun hats for the dog on the go.

But speaking of dogs on the go, or at least dogs that need to go, Ken didn't immediately intuit that the Barkery wasn't the kind of place where you could just lift your leg over a cashmere doggy bed and do your business. Thankfully, we were able to yank him fast enough so that he hit a leather "Barkalounger" instead. We were grateful, since leather is so much easier to clean than cashmere. Pets worn out from all their shopping also enjoy spendy gourmet cookies and pastries, each in a fancy foil cup, displayed behind a glass case.

We watched in amazement as shoppers snapped up boots and silver heart necklaces for their pooches, but we had to leave quickly when Ken decided to use his teeth to examine an ivory Damask pillow with brush fringe accents. No way would I spend ninety-five bucks on a chew toy.

I confess that one winter, we did expand Ken's wardrobe from only a collar and rabies tag to a trench coat. We hoped that, shielded from the elements, he might be willing to walk in the rain he despises for more than thirty seconds. Although he looked dapper in his coat, he also looked depressed, as if we had inflicted the deepest possible insult. It's really a shame, though. When he wore it and also had a bone hanging out of his mouth, he was a dead ringer for Peter Sellers as Inspector Clouseau.

No doubt that my neighbor, Josie, human companion of

the dog, Molly, with issues, would strongly disapprove of our having exploited our dog, however briefly, by dressing him up for our own amusement. Do I care? Trench coat aside, I laugh my head off just thinking that Josie takes her dog to a therapist. Maybe if Molly wasn't forced to wear a kimono to therapy, her issues might go away.

Advice to Airline Passengers: Don't Forget the Passports or the Popcorn

My family and I have just returned from an exciting adventure in international travel. From the first moment, we displayed the kind of calm serenity that is the hallmark of all Gruen travel adventures:

Husband: "Do you have the plane tickets?"

Me: "Yes, I have the tickets."

Husband: "Do you have all the passports?"

Me: "You already asked me that twice."

Husband: "I just want to be thorough. Did you say you have the tickets?"

Me: "YES! I have all the passports AND all the tickets!"

Husband: "Do we have all the children?"

Me: "You better climb in back and count them."

By the time we located all our children hiding under our thirteen suitcases and ten carry-on bags, we had arrived at the airport and offered ourselves up to the indignities of modern air travel. These begin with the strip poker antics in the airport security line. First you lose your shoes, then your belt, then your hat, if you dared to wear one. You tirelessly whip out photo ID to officious TSA agents stationed every five feet all the way to the boarding gate, careful to refrain from making jokes about hidden bombs, even if the jokes are exceedingly funny. These are heavy sacrifices indeed.

After slogging through security lines, we were perilously close to boarding time. Still, one must manage priorities, so we made a mad dash to the food court to buy sticky buns that were so gigantic that the flight attendant threatened to check them as luggage. By the time we settled into our ruler-width airplane seats, I already looked like my passport photo.

Naturally, the flight was over-booked and under-oxygenated, although additional oxygen was available for only twenty dollars per passenger. I pressed the button to recline my seat, instantly breaking the nose of the passenger behind me. "Hey!" the bloodied little man in 29F shouted. I was mortified to have hurt a fellow human being, yet I couldn't help but worry: Who would sue me first, the passenger or the airline? Equally worrisome was how soon they'd serve coffee to go with my giant sticky bun. I was hungry.

Seventeen hours later, when we were still airborne and several time zones from our destination, I no longer resembled my passport photo. Instead, I looked like Danny DeVito's passport photo. I attribute this to flying "economy class," a condition with uncanny resemblance to what my great-grandparents endured when they rode steerage in boats bringing them to the Land of the Free and the home of the all-you-can-eat Sunday buffet brunch. Let's face it: When someone who is barely five feet, four inches tall (and that's when I'm feeling confident) cannot stow both her carry-on bag and her feet under the same chair, how comfortable can everybody else be, especially that giraffe of a man in 14B?

I had planned to follow the expert advice about getting up every two hours and walking around to avoid circulation problems. But this involved climbing over and waking a sleeping spouse to rouse my kneecaps from their locked and upright position above the carry-on bag. I limited this activity to times when I urgently needed the lavatory, the same lavatory whose occupant refused to surrender the premises. After only a half hour, I got knocked in the face when the woman opened the door.

No doubt it's wise that they keep the curtain drawn between those of us flying steerage, um, I meant to say economy, and those who sit in splendor in their First Class Barcaloungers. After so many hours being stuffed together like sausages, who knows what rebellion might result if we saw the pampered class getting shiatsu massage and French cuisine prepared by the First Class chef?

Once I got stuck behind a flight attendant wheeling her little cart from which she was flinging hot towels at passengers. These towels were our *hors d'oeuvres* to the little meal they would offer for sale on their next circuit of the plane, and no doubt as tasty. I cooled my heels until the flight attendant had flung her last hot towel at my husband, sitting in the last row of the plane, but became faint with hunger as I passed row 24G, where a woman was happily chomping away at popcorn brought from home. She ignored my longing looks, and I wished I had not devoured my entire sticky bun eight hours ago. Clearly, it was every passenger for herself on this flight. Back in my seat, I found my meal still a bit frozen, but no matter. I had plenty of time to wait until it defrosted, since the label on the tray said the meal wouldn't expire for another twenty-four months. I hoped we would have landed by then.

There is much more to tell about our adventures in international travel. For example, we experienced the distinct thrill of being driven around by native taxi drivers careening us around at 140 kilometers an hour, seemingly out to kill us for no reason whatsoever. There were also my ongoing efforts to convert foreign currency into dollars and, failing that, blithely overpaying for everything. But the good news was that I discovered that I weigh a lot less on the metric system, and I used this information to my benefit at the morning breakfast buffet.

My parting advice for any of you contemplating any long flights in steerage class is: Don't forget your passports, and whatever you do, bring your own popcorn.

I, the Juror

Like most everyone I know, I had managed to slink out of jury duty each time the Los Angeles County court system tried to nab me. Californians used to wriggle out of jury duty for any number of reasons, such as being a primary caretaker of children, or having difficulty getting transportation to the courthouse because you are locked up in Folsom Prison.

These neat loopholes meant that most juries comprise people who had no job to miss, no kids to care for (that they knew of), and no reason to be anywhere at any time. After these juries issued a string of embarrassing "not guilty" verdicts for hardened criminals who all but left their business cards at the scene of the crimes, the state decided to get tough. Now nearly all citizens with a pulse must serve, no matter how pressing their duties to write humor columns.

I relished the idea of being chosen foreperson and persuading my colleagues on the jury to agree with me that we should throw the bum into prison. However, it would be best for my schedule if I could carefully weigh the evidence and render this objective, impartial and informed decision while still making my 3:45 p.m. carpool.

Everyone at the courthouse downtown looked guilty to me, especially that attorney wearing a pair of blindingly shiny $500 shoes. An hour later, a judge introduced himself to the hundreds of us waiting in the jury waiting room, and quizzed us on our knowledge of California criminal law. One prospective juror, desperately in need of a shave and a clean pair of pants, displayed uncanny knowledge about the legal differences between grand theft, armed robbery, and how many times you could fail the breathalyzer test before a DUI gets slapped on your record.

After our lesson in jurisprudence, we watched a film featuring proud citizens who reminisced with pride about gaining increased self-esteem, a pay raise, and even bagging more dates after having served on jury duty. The judge reminded us that at this very moment, Americans were risking their lives in a war overseas while others were heroically helping with hurricane rescue efforts. "*You* just need to sit here and wait to be summoned to a jury while watching TV, so don't complain," he said.

We waited to be called. And waited. Pretty soon, I had read two years' worth of *Needlepoint Monthly* and *Contact Lens Spectrum* magazines.

If I didn't get called by five o'clock, I would be free until next year. With only minutes left before I could make a break for it, I was called to a courtroom on the seventh floor, along with a dozen others. There, the judge thanked us for waiting the entire day, then told us to go home and come back the next morning. One look at the defendant convinced me he was guilty. Why, his brow was so furrowed with worry you could have planted a row of corn on his forehead. Could I shake this bias if I were a juror? With decades of making snap decisions so deeply ingrained, it would be a challenge.

The next day, I became one of two alternates. This didn't entitle me to sit in the jury box, a keenly felt disappointment. But if the attorneys kept booting other jurors out of the box like contestants on *Survivor*, I might get to move up the jury food chain, perhaps even achieving my dream of becoming foreperson.

The prosecuting attorney was a major windbag, but at least my fellow jurors were an entertaining bunch, representing a typically eclectic cross-section of Los Angeles careerists: We had two screenwriters, a post-production set designer, a film editor, a wardrobe designer, a key grip, and an accountant.

At lunch, juror #8 warned me, "You're history. You'll be dismissed as soon as we get back." I knew he was right. When questioned about my beliefs about the case, I admitted that it would be hard for me to view the defendant objectively. The guy was accused of four counts of threatening behavior against a young woman, which reminded me of a close friend who also once ended up on the wrong side of a bad man. This was a different man and different circumstances, but when the judge asked if any of us had experienced a situation similar to this or knew someone who did, I had to answer honestly.

I don't blame the remaining jurors for their impatience. They had seen fluent English speakers in the elevator suddenly pretend their English was no good while answering questions in the jury box, dullards who seemed to have no opinion about anything, overly analytical college students who were probably dismissed for being overly analytical, and scores of others dismissed for reasons that remain a mystery.

Juror #8 should have called odds in Vegas. He had successfully predicted the booting of twenty-four previous prospective jurors, and was right about my dismissal, too. Still, I couldn't help but wonder what would have happened had I remained on the jury, and whether I could have made foreperson, although I know that Juror #2, the set designer, would have given me a run for my money.

If I thought I was off the hook for dispensing justice, however, I was wrong. A few weeks later, my friend and neighbor Sally asked me to accompany her to "Doggy Court" to testify on behalf of Bubbles, the Chihuahua. It was something of a comedown from the Criminal Court building downtown, but it was something.

At only three pounds and six inches tall, Bubbles is a sorry excuse for a dog. In my opinion, any dog small enough to fit in a shoe is more an annoyance than a pet. You can never see them without binoculars, and end up stepping on them by accident, inducing guilt. But Sally loves this tiny thing boundlessly, and besides, Bubbles has another redeeming quality in that she is good friends with our dog, Ken. So when our neighbor, Marvin the Misanthrope, reported Bubbles to the police for her incessant barking, I could hardly abandon them in their time of need.

Marvin the Misanthrope is one of those weird guys who does not even pretend to be friendly. If one day he turned out to be an ax murderer, no one on the block would exclaim in shock to a reporter, "But he always helped me dig my car out from the snow and delivered meals to shut-ins!" Instead they'd say, "Well, that explains it."

Marvin complained repeatedly to Sally about Bubbles' habit of barking, which was not an unusual trait in a dog. Admittedly, Bubbles can be pretty loud, and I have long suspected that she has a bit of a Napoleonic complex. In fact, Bubbles is not much larger than a napoleon (the bakery kind). But Marvin didn't appreciate Bubbles' yappish efforts to protect the neighborhood through baying vigorously at every passing car, truck or pedestrian. Nor did he appreciate Sally's efforts to keep the Chihuahua quiet. He just wanted her to shut up.

With a brain not much larger than a pea, Bubbles did not understand that she was driving Marvin the Misanthrope mad. Knowing that Marvin was losing patience, Sally brought him a home-cooked meal and freshly baked chocolate chip cookies by way of apology, but—prepare yourselves—he refused them, proving that in addition to being a miserable wretch of a human being, Marvin is also an idiot. Everyone in the neighborhood knows that Sally is a fantastic cook.

Sally's "food for peace" program backfired, and the next week, she received a summons to court in an action brought by Marvin. Bubbles' fate hung in the balance.

"You've got to help me!" Sally pleaded as we walked our dogs together, trying to avoid leash burn as Bubbles and Ken wrapped themselves around our legs. "I have nightmares about Marvin dressed like the Wicked Witch of the West, screeching, 'I'll get you, my little pretty, and your little dog, too!' Then he grabs Bubbles and throws her in a dirty backpack and drives off while the authorities just stand by. I won't be able to cope if anything happens to Bubbles." The image of Marvin wearing a witch's cape and pointy hat was chilling enough. Even I was moved by the thought that this minuscule scrap of a dog might be taken from Sally because of Marvin's malevolence. Besides, with whom would Ken spend his lazy afternoons if not with Bubbles?

"Don't worry, Sally. Marvin won't stand a chance against us."

We walked by his house, the only one on the block with no lawn. Even grass could not grow in the inhospitable environment inhabited by Miserable Marvin. I went home and typed up a petition, which asked neighbors to affirm Bubbles' exemplary character and Marvin's bad one. Further, the petition stated that Marvin's refusal to landscape was driving property values down and therefore the government should seize his property under eminent domain. Other than one neighbor who was convinced I was really trying to collect money for a save-the-endangered-mollusk fund, I had no trouble gathering more than a dozen signatures.

On the day of the hearing, I picked up Sally and Bubbles,

who was smartly attired in a new pink leopard-print collar with two bells and matching fringed sweater set. There was a decided chill in the air even before we entered the room to face Bubbles' nemesis.

Marvin was surprised to see me. "I never thought that you'd turn on me like this," Marvin said, looking hurt.

"You gave me no choice, Marvin," I said. "Your bald front yard is bad enough, but when you reported Bubbles to the police, you went too far."

The judge called us into a small, sterile looking room that did not exactly radiate an aura of justice. However, he and Bubbles hit it off immediately, and the judge allowed her to lick his hand with her flyspeck of a tongue. Marvin could hardly contain his revulsion.

Marvin recited a long litany of dates, times and durations of Bubbles' alleged barkfests. Then he asked the judge permission to play a videotape that he promised would seal Bubbles' fate. As Sally and I held our breaths, and even Bubbles, sensing that something was terribly amiss, whimpered, her pointy little ears suddenly rearing back in fear. Marvin had secretly mounted a camera from his own den of depravity next door, filming Sally's yard, or at least one wall of it, to indict Bubbles.

Marvin rolled the tape, barely containing his excitement. We all stared intently at the wall of Sally's house. A minute or two passed, but no damning barks were heard.

"It's coming, don't worry," said Marvin, worriedly.

"Marvin, I don't hear any barking on this tape," said the judge after a few more moments of silence.

"I promise you it's here!" Marvin's voice began to crack. "I stayed up all night watching this! Just wait!"

Sally and I exchanged glances with the judge, and even Bubbles began to relax. I wanted to laugh at Marvin's utter humiliation, but he was too creepy to risk doing so. I bit my lip instead, and it was beginning to hurt.

Several more excruciating minutes passed, during which Marvin's tape revealed absolutely nothing except that if you looked hard enough, you could see an area where Sally's paint was beginning to crack from sun exposure. Finally, the judge's patience ran out.

"Please turn it off, Marvin," the judge ordered.

"There must be something wrong with the audio!" Marvin was dangerously close to the edge, and I pushed my chair farther away from him in the uncomfortably small room. What if Marvin was packing heat? Where were all the armed bailiffs when you needed them? I hated to think that during my first real chance to do my bit for justice, I would be blown away by a nutcase, simply defending a Chihuahua dressed like a rock star. Somehow, that would seem like a waste.

On the theory that it's always best to hit your enemy when he's already low, I chose that moment to offer my petition as exhibit A in the case. The judge allowed me to read the petition and show him all the signatories. Bubbles was cleared of the canine charges against her. The case was closed.

As Marvin angrily shoved his camera into his bag, the judge said, "You're lucky you don't live next door to me, Marvin. I've got two Rottweilers." And with that, Marvin turned to Sally and warned, "I'm not through with you yet! I'll take this to an appellate court!" Then he stormed out of the room.

Bubbles gave the judge a final lick of thanks before we left. Sally and I peered out the window to make sure Marvin had gone before we dared to go out to the parking lot. After all, Bubbles was not likely to offer much protection, and as usual I had forgotten to buy pepper spray.

On the way home, we stopped at Pets-a-Rama to buy new dog treats and bones for Bubbles and Ken. That afternoon, we hosted a party in Sally's yard for all the dogs in the neighborhood. And just for posterity, we caught all the festivities on tape.

J.K. Rowling, the Senior Ladies' Lunch Club, and Me

Like millions of other kids in the known universe, my daughter is a full-fledged Harry Pottermaniac. Still, I should have known better than to suggest that she write a book report on J.K. Rowling for school.

"Did you know that J.K. Rowling had three books on the *New York Times* bestseller list at the same time?" my daughter asked as I sat paying bills. "Did you know that she's sold more than a quarter of a *billion* books and that Harry Potter has been translated into twenty-five different languages? Hey, Mommy, have *your* books been translated into any other languages? Not even one?"

Don't get me wrong: Rowling's a wonderful storyteller, but as a writer impossibly remote from her magical success, this much detail began to grate. I slid away from my daughter and her all-Rowling, all-the-time broadcast to check my e-mail. Happily, I discovered an invitation to speak to a women's club. Aha! Apparently J.K. Rowling isn't the only author in demand!

My enthusiasm for the gig waned when I learned that the average age of club members was around eighty-years-old. Painful experience had taught me that speaking to the aged is no walk on the shuffleboard court. The audience tends to nod off, even during your funniest riffs. (This probably doesn't happen to Rowling, since her audience is mostly naturally caffeinated ten-year-olds.) Second, the elderly don't laugh as vigorously as younger folks, making even the wittiest presentations appear less than successful. On the other hand, I didn't want to be accused of being ageist. How would I feel if, when I am old, younger speakers snubbed me as a less worthy audience?

With trepidation, I agreed to speak to the club. At the meeting, I was distressed to learn that they wanted me to speak during dessert. Could even Jerry Seinfeld compete with trays of double-fudge layer cake being passed under the noses of his audience? I wedged myself into the middle of the room between a walker and a wheelchair and began, speaking loudly. I was winding up to my first punch line when there was an uproar.

"The deaf people are over here!" shouted a lady in pink at the far end of the room.

"Yeah! You need to stand over here!" agreed another octogenarian.

"We can't hear you!" I stopped just short of my punch line, kept smiling, and sidled over to the more intensely hearing-impaired corner of the room, where I tried not to lose my mojo. I resumed shouting.

"Medical researchers now predict that one day people will live to about 120," I bellowed, "but they say we'll probably need replacement parts. Can you imagine? We'll all be shopping at places like 'Bed, Breasts and Beyond' . . . ."

"Tell me what your doctor said about your gallstones later, Betty!" I heard a woman insist. "The nice lady is trying to talk now!"

"Are you sure this is Sweet 'N Low?" another blurted out as her coffee was served. I continued gamely on despite the rash of outbursts. When I joked about a famous male cookbook author known as "The Naked Chef," one club member dared to ask me about my sex life. These gals were a tough crowd.

I couldn't wait to finish and sign and sell my books. But instead of capitalizing on whatever enthusiasm I had generated, the club president stalled the book sale until she had read congratulatory proclamations to club members enjoying birthdays that month. Each proclamation was approximately the length of a Senate appropriations bill. When the birthday salutations were complete, I held my special book-signing pen with anticipation.

"Let's sing some songs, shall we?" the president said. It was more a command than a suggestion. My pen sat motionless.

The women launched into a medley of songs, mostly in Yiddish, about long-lost love and the old country. My heart softened for the women, but I lost patience when one woman hefted herself up and then belted out several favorite songs of her own—in Hungarian. Another half-hour later, those who were ambulatory stood up and we all sang "God Bless America."

I finally sold a few books and basked in the glory of the compliments that came my way. It was more than I expected, since only half of them seemed to be paying attention. I thanked my hosts and dashed off, making it just in time to pick up my afternoon carpool. Not surprisingly, my daughter was exploding with new facts about the fabulous J.K. Rowling.

"Mommy, did you know that J.K. Rowling read to 16,000 people at the Toronto Skydome?"

"That's nothing," I replied hoarsely, my voice now shot. "I just spoke to forty elderly Jewish women who kept interrupting to sing songs in Yiddish and to talk about their gallstones. You tell me: Which was the bigger challenge?"

It's true, Rowling may now be richer even than the Queen

of England, but I was happy to learn that she once said, "I am an extraordinarily lucky person, doing what I love best in the world. The greatest reward is the enthusiasm of the readers."

I *knew* we had something in common.

It's Not Easy Being Boring

My agent was at it again. Always trolling for ways to nudge my career forward, he asked if I could please try to think of something exciting in my past that would prove grist for the publishing mill. More exciting, that is, than parenting a passel of kids in the age of reality TV, international terrorism, Internet smut, and other newfangled inventions.

"You've got to face facts," he said. "Publishers like celebrities, and since you're not Paris Hilton, or even Paris Hilton's dog, you need a fresh angle. Talent alone just won't cut it anymore."

"That will come as a shock to Paris and her dog," I noted.

"Don't be cynical. Crime sells, as long as you're the real deal. There's nothing lower than someone pretending to have a rap sheet when all they've ever really done is rap," he said, oozing disapproval over these ersatz criminals. "Besides, you don't want Oprah taking you to the woodshed for making things up. If you're going to show needle marks, they better not be from Botox, *capiche?* Think hard: Haven't you done anything illegal in the past?"

Dutifully, I sat and thought. Suddenly, a shameful memory rose to the top of the cerebellum. "I can't discuss it," I said. "It's too humiliating."

"The more humiliating the better!" he said. "Come on, out with it!"

So I confessed: At age seven, I shoplifted two squares of

Bazooka bubble gum from the gas station's mini-mart. I couldn't sleep for two nights after.

My agent was unimpressed. "I had assumed you had shown more literary promise in your early childhood. Okay, work with me here. Maybe crime isn't your game. How about family dysfunction? Everybody has that! Who in your family was alcoholic? Abusive? Were you molested? I'm sure you were. Traumatized by a psychotic uncle who later had a sex-change operation? I know an editor who'd pay big money now for a story about a psychotic uncle who had a sex-change operation."

I thought again. My childhood was not pain-free, but did I want to spill the sludge in the open market? Besides, who would want to plunk down $24.95 to read about Great-Aunt Lilly and her delusions that she was really Catherine the Great? How-to books sell well, but what did I really know, anyway, other than 100 ways to make low-fat desserts that taste . . . low-fat? I walked around the room to wake up more brain matter. Other than the time Jimmy Dougherty tried to kiss me after school in the fourth grade, I couldn't think of any situation where I had felt so miserably exploited, abused, and near death. I wasn't sure that would qualify to get me on *Larry King Live*.

"You're pushing me here," I said, "but once I got an obscene phone call from a guy with a foot fetish."

He leaned in closer. "Now we're getting somewhere. What happened?"

"I hung up on him, obviously!"

He threw up his hands in exasperation. "You never miss an opportunity to miss an opportunity, you know that? Do me a favor. Next time you get an obscene phone call, at least have the courtesy to meet the guy. Talk to him. See what's driving his voyeurism. You could be sitting on an inspirational story of obsessive infatuations, forgiveness, redemption, and triumph. I see movie rights also."

As he spoke, I realized with dismay how boring my life had been. How could I compete with women who have been kidnaped by crazed heavy metal guitarists and dropped in the Amazon, or women who adopted fourteen special needs children, all from Moldavia? They got book contracts. But unless I wanted my writing career to sputter to a halt, I'd have to do something equally bold and adventurous. Unfortunately, my current commitments involving constant grocery shopping, chauffeuring kids and laundry don't allow much time for foreign exploits.

"You probably were so traumatized in your childhood that you've covered it up," my agent said helpfully.

Finally, an optimistic note. "You must be right! I'll hire a past-lives regression analyst who can help me remember whatever it was that happened," I said. "If I'm lucky, I'll discover that in a previous life I was a CIA operative whose tryst with a South American dictator nearly led to the collapse of the entire banana export industry. Or perhaps I'd recall an existence where I'd been a quiet, dutiful Amish jam-maker who suddenly released my inner crazy, hitchhiked away from Pennsylvania and went to Hollywood, where I became a Playboy bunny."

"Now you're talking. By the way, one of my authors just discovered that her husband's been secretly gay during their entire marriage, her son was just diagnosed with Tourette syndrome, and she developed a very rare, weird rash on her hip that no dermatologist can cure."

"We all can't share in her good fortune," I said. "If the past lives regression therapy doesn't pan out, how about a memoir by a traditional mom who is desperately trying to maintain her grip on reality in a world where America's most-watched TV moms are chopping off fingers of ex-lovers, checking themselves into psych hospitals, and passing out drunk in bars while their kids' birthday parties are hosted by mom's sexaholic boyfriends? As a boring mom, I'm an oppressed minority!"

"You could be onto something there," he said, pacing the room. "But when you write it, can you at least try to develop a rare, yet curable blood disorder?"

Oprah's Memo to God

To: God
From: Oprah
Subject: Would love to have you on the show

Dear God,

First, I want you to know that You are very special to me. I have believed in You all of my life, from my humble beginnings in that ramshackle Mississippi backwater where we were so poor I barely had shoes (let alone a closet full of Manolo Blahniks), to where I am today, the most influential African-American woman in the known universe, and perhaps even in galaxies beyond. I thank You for believing in me and for making me so incredibly shrewd, yet relatable at the same time.

Although I really appreciate all that You have done, it's pretty clear that You are not as powerful as You once were, whereas I am becoming more powerful each day.

For example, when I recommend a new bra, tens of millions of women stampede the malls, searching for that exact style. They will not sleep at night until they get that bra. When I recommend a book, they won't have a moment's peace until they read it. Decorators across the country were suddenly booked a year in advance after I broadcast the show, "Is your home décor stuck in the 80s?"

Ask Yourself, Lord, do You still command that kind of authority?

I'll admit, when reporters first asked me, "Oprah, are you God?" I denied it. First, that would have been arrogant. But false modesty is useless.

Maybe if You had started a web site, or had asked me to recommend a really shrewd PR firm, my ministry wouldn't have grown larger than Yours. However, it never pays to look back in regret. I've got a gazillion people watching my television show (check newspaper listings for local air time), more millions who read *O, The Oprah Magazine*, featuring Me on the cover in a different outfit and a different sized body each month. I've got them listening to my new twenty-four-hour satellite radio shows. I even have my own Angel Network.

God, You taught me to dream big. And I listened to that voice, and embraced the message. I even realized that the whole "Oprah for President" business was just a ruse, a way for You to get me to realize my full transformational potential. Now I see that You not only wanted me to be God-like in my ability to give away Pontiac G6s to everyone in my audience, get Christiane Amanpour or Ralph Lauren on my set at the snap of my fingers, and order the entire nation to send money to help the victims of Darfur. It was to actually become God.

Even for Me, this was heady stuff. When I began to think of the implications, I needed to sit quietly with a cup of herbal tea. I asked my staff not to disturb Me, even though they were eager to show Me the photos of Myself for the next month's magazine cover, where I look stunning in size six (can you believe it?) camel slacks and a divine chocolate shearling jacket. This was big. Bigger than getting Faith Hill to divulge her recipe for cornbread on my show. Bigger than Tom Cruise's moon bounce on my couch. Bigger, even, than the show when we revealed the last pair of tweezers you'll ever need.

Besides, you are probably feeling a little burned out after so many thousands of years of being God. Who wouldn't? And let's face facts: Nobody can stay in the limelight forever. I feel total serenity with my new mission, and my leap into the evolutionary light. I see that you have done for me the exact same thing I try to do for My own parishioners. You have allowed Me to discover my truest potential. I thank you for that.

So I accept. I will end all speculation and announce to the world that I am, in fact, God. I have already confided this to a few close friends and promised them that it won't change anything between us. Most felt relieved, but one did ask, since I was now God, and probably would no longer have use for my estimated $1.4 billion net worth, could I throw a little moola his way? I said, sure, no sweat. I even tossed in a navy bucket hat with the Oprah Book Club logo embroidered on it. If God can't be generous, who can?

How can I thank you for leading me on this extraordinary journey? The most meaningful thing I can think of is to invite you as a guest on *The Oprah Winfrey Show*. I'm sure you realize that most people would volunteer to become double amputees for an opportunity of this kind. And if the audience really connects with you, we may have you back on a regular basis. (I assume frequent travel won't pose any difficulties.) Dr. Phil started that way, look what happened! A TV show, best-selling books, the works. It could happen to you, too.

Unfortunately, our schedule is kind of booked for the next few months. There's just no way we can bump the upcoming shows, "Are you a closet racist?" and "Gospel singers addicted to porn." We could potentially book you for a week from Thursday, but I have to warn you that if Parvez Musharraf's schedule opens up, you'll get bumped. He promised to share his secret recipe for spicy hummus, and I for one just can't wait. In the meantime, since you will be looking for a new line of work, you may want to sign up to receive a daily e-mailed inspirational messages, or take our online quiz, "How Can I Become My Best Self?"

In closing, I am giving you my top-secret e-mail address. Please keep it confidential. You have no idea how many computer servers will go down if this info gets out. But feel free to drop me a line anytime, especially if you meet any transgendered people who have managed to lose weight and keep it off. These folks have been maddeningly hard to find.

So thank you. You have been so supportive, and I'll never forget it. Remember, let your inner dreams rise with the sun!

Imagine Peace,

Oprah

The Fabrically Challenged Female

I hate to sound strident, but discrimination against women is really becoming unbearable.

How else can we explain the phenomenon of the blouse that thinks it's a handkerchief and NC-17-rated jeans? Health care isn't the only area where women are being denied coverage these days. It wouldn't surprise me if a cabal of cruel HMO administrators has clandestinely agreed to deny coverage to women's abdomens, claiming that belly buttons—both "innies" and "outies"—are preexisting conditions.

Women have often complained of hitting the "glass ceiling" in the workplace when they were denied career promotions simply because of their gender. But when women hit the glass ceiling, at least they weren't in the humiliating position of having to tuck their *décolletage* back inside their six-inch tube tops while massaging their banged-up heads on their way out the door. Today, women have hit a much lower ceiling, one that shows the whole world their butterfly-tattooed backsides.

Don't women deserve more than a few miserly yards of material for their entire wardrobes? Are we in the throes of a national fabric shortage? The results of this situation are not pretty. Yesterday, I saw another poor victim of this vast textile conspiracy in the market. Poor thing had been reduced to stuffing herself into barely-there jeans and a top with only one strap. She tottered in four-inch heels in the frozen foods aisle, and I feared that her bosom, amply revealed, would be flash frozen as soon as she opened the door to reach for the rhubarb. Looking furtively to the left and right, she began to reach down for the bag. Then, hearing my cart turn down her aisle, she suddenly straightened up and deftly tucked herself back into her top.

As I often do when I meet handicapped people in the market, I offered to help. "Need me to get that for you?"

"Oh yes, thanks. I'll take two packages of the rhubarb. While you're at it, get me a package of strawberries, no sugar added."

I tossed the items in her cart. "Anything else you need as long as I'm here? Frozen fishsticks maybe, or some Lean Cuisines?"

She thought for a moment. "No, but would you mind coming with me to aisle twelve? I need some fabric softener, and it's hard to reach that top shelf in these things."

"Let's go," I said, always happy to help a fellow citizen. "But listen, why are you wearing these clothes if they're such trouble?"

She then looked at me strangely, as if I had just told her that my pig could fly. "You've got to be kidding," she said. "These are the hottest styles right now. I don't want to look like I just fell off the turnip truck. No offense or anything," she added, after eyeing my below-the-knee skirt and wrinkling her nose just a tad.

While we pushed our carts together in amiable companionship, I saw that the woman's fashions were a threat to public order. One man heading toward us became so distracted when he saw her he banged his cart right into a stack of Parkay margarine, upsetting the entire display. The produce manager started putting bananas in the mango section. Fortunately, I had a tissue handy so he could mop up the dribble from his chin. And, even though she was eligible to check out in the ten-items-or-less line and I had an overflowing cart, she received multiple offers of help to her car, some of them even from store personnel. I was only asked the usual perfunctory "credit or debit?" question, but no one offered to help me to my car, even though by this time my overladen cart had a sprained wheel, and was trying to go in opposite directions at once.

I didn't need any man to help me lug my groceries into the car, even though I was hauling a twenty-gallon vat of laundry detergent. Not only was I stronger than my fabrically-challenged friend, I was fully clothed.

The Price Is Never Right

I never would have suspected that when my friend Donna bought her new area rug, it would doom our friendship. And yet, sometimes it's these small encounters over trifling economic transactions that can have unexpected ripple effects, upsetting the entire chain of human relationships. Sadly, this is what happened with Donna and me.

I should have seen it coming. Telling Donna about any purchase I made has always been a mistake, because she was habitually compelled to let me know that however much I had spent on something, she had got hers cheaper. Usually a lot cheaper.

Take the rug, for example, which is exactly what Donna did for only fifteen bucks from a guy selling them on a lonely street lot in town. When Donna discovered that I had bought my area rug from an actual store, a pained look spread across her face. Donna's philosophy of shopping is, if you bought it from a place with a roof on it, you paid too much. After my confession, Donna predictably grilled me about how much I paid for it. As usual, I lied. But I did so only for her own benefit. I didn't think Donna couldn't stomach the news that I had plunked down more than two hundred greenbacks for it. What else can you expect from a woman whose hobby is watching the Home Shopping Network and shouting at the television that only a fool would pay four dollars for a set of ten gutter screws or seventy-five bucks for a four-foot-tall lighted deer?

The Women's Daily Irony Supplement

It's always been like this with Donna and me. Years ago when I showed her my new dining set, she managed to worm the price out of me, then collapsed into one of my overpriced chairs and told me that for the same price, she got an entire table, two extension leaves and chairs for twelve. But what else would you expect from a woman who buys nearly everything at liquidation sales of merchandise seized by the IRS? All of Donna's furnishings and jewelry once belonged either to drug warlords or tax delinquents who had their stuff carted off by the government, only to have people like Donna swoop down on it, pouncing on the best deals.

As a bargain hunter, I'll always be bush league compared to Donna. When she saw that I bought my kids a plastic jungle gym from Target, she burst with the information that she had found hers at a garage sale for twenty bucks. In fact, I realized that there is nothing in Donna's life that wasn't discovered at a clearance outlet, garage sale, or by the side of the freeway. I once tried to play her game, and hoped she'd be proud when I showed her some fabric sizing and canned green beans I bought at the 99-cent store. But Donna trumped me even here, gleefully telling me about the little-known existence of a 98-cent store, where she buys all her non-perishable food items and detergent.

Donna even met her husband through a personal ad in the *Recycler* newspaper. The ad read, "Original owner. Chassis like new. Great for off-roading. Make an offer!" Finally, Donna had met the man of her dreams. After all, how many men come with their own smog certifications these days, anyway?

But the way she rubbed my nose in her area rug, so to speak, was the final straw. I have my pride. And while I like a sale as much as anyone (well, except for Donna) I don't feel obligated to commit hari-kari if I sometimes pay retail, a word that makes every fiber of Donna's being recoil in horror and disgust.

It wouldn't surprise me if Donna's profiled in that book, *The Millionaire Next Store*. She makes a good living, but she's never paid more than thirty bucks for anything in her life, including her major appliances. I've decided that all this competition over bargains is just not worth it. Besides, I think the Home Shopping Network's price for the gutter screws wasn't bad. I'm going to go turn on the set now and see if they're still available. And if Donna happens to drop by unexpectedly to lord it over me on some new purchase, mum's the word on where I got the lighted deer.

And They Wonder Why Voter Turnout Is So Low

When the phone rang, my heart skipped a beat. I had a feeling that it must be an editor from a swanky New York magazine calling to offer me a fat check for my work.

"Hello?" I answered in my seasoned, professional writer's voice.

"Ms. Gurend?"

A New York editor would not have mangled my name like that. I was instantly deflated.

"It's *Gruen,* but yes, you're speaking with her." Maybe it was an editorial intern.

"Oh, my apologies, Ms. Bruin, I'm calling from the National Gasbag Senatorial Campaign and we want to thank you for your prior support."

I knew what was coming next. The Gasbag Party and even, inexplicably, the Malcontent Party, had been hammering me with torrents of letters that were written MOSTLY IN CAPITAL LETTERS SO I UNDERSTOOD THAT OUR COUNTRY'S VERY SURVIVAL HUNG IN THE BALANCE! MY FAILURE TO SEND AN ADDITIONAL $500, $1,000, OR WHATEVER I COULD SEND TODAY MIGHT PLUNGE OUR NATION INTO THE ABYSS! MY SUPPORT—NOW—

WOULD HELP PREVENT OUR NATION FROM BEING FLOODED BY POORLY REGULATED CANADIAN PRESCRIPTION DRUGS AND CHEAP FURNITURE MADE IN MACAU, THUS THREATENING AMERICAN JOBS.

I had to put a stop to this.

"Yes, but you see I have already given to the Gasbag Party and I'm afraid . . . ."

"Ms. Strewin we really do appreciate your support but with only forty-six days until the election it is absolutely *vital* that you give us more money for our next television ads showing that the Malcontent Party candidate failed to show up for track practice in high school and also refuses to release his immunization records from seventh grade. This is a tight race, and we are targeting these television ads in key swing states, such as Alaska and Rhode Island, which are worth seven electoral votes. Can I put you down for a modest $2,000 donation?"

"Look, I'd like to help, but I think both parties need to move on from issues dating back to when the candidates still had braces on their teeth. I'd like to hear more about today's issues, such as national security and cursing in public. I need to hang up now."

"But Ms. Truman . . . ."

Five minutes later, the phone rang again. Perhaps this was an actual business call.

"Hello, Ms. Groomin?"

I didn't have a good feeling about this, either.

"It's *Gruen*. What can I do for you?"

"Oh, I'm so sorry Ms. Grootin, I'm Terri from the Committee to Elect the Malcontent Candidates and I want to thank you for your past support."

"Sorry, Terri, I haven't voted the Malcontent ticket in years. You need to update your records."

"But Ms. Groanen I beg you to reconsider. If the Gasbag Party has their way you can kiss your civil rights goodbye!"

I hated to cut her to the quick, but these calls were getting annoying.

"Look, I understand you have a hard job to do, especially with your candidate slumping in the polls, but . . . ."

"Our candidate is *not* slumping in the polls! Our internal tracking data show she has a three percentage poll lead among swing voters in Wyoming."

You had to feel sorry for all these swing voters. Imagine all the calls *they* had to fend off, with everyone and his or her brother-in-law on the political landscape taking their electoral temperature every five minutes.

"I have to go now, Terri. Have a nice day."

"Wait! Just do me a favor and check out our Web site. If you vote for our candidate, we will personally pick you up and take you to your local voting precinct, and give you orange juice and cookies afterward."

"Thanks, Terri. Perhaps you can donate your orange juice to the Red Cross at their next blood drive. Oh-oh, the UPS man is here. Also the plumber and an auditor from the IRS."

I hung up before she could direct me to any other Web sites or tantalize me with even more exotic door prizes, such as cranberry juice. Frazzled, I walked to the kitchen for a restorative cup of coffee and a large Reese's Peanut Butter Cup.

Returning to my desk, I savored my coffee and practiced pronouncing my last name, which had become confusing, even to me. The phone rang again. At this point, I'd settle for a call from a telemarketer trying to sell me a free estimate on home remodeling. Anything but another political sales pitch.

"Hewwo?" This is what happens when you answer the phone

with your teeth an inch deep in peanut butter. There was a pause, and then I listened as a recorded message urged me to vote the Malcontent or ex-felons would move in next door to me. I slammed the phone down. I had two hours' respite before the phone rang again. I didn't recognize the caller ID, and made the mistake of answering anyway.

"Ms. Geruvin?"

This couldn't be happening, except that it was. "It's Gruen, *Gruen,* do you hear? Who's calling?"

"It's Chad, from the National Piffle Party. Would you sign a petition to allow our candidate to appear on the ballot in your state?"

"Hang it up, Chad," I said. "Third-party candidates are a waste. In fact, today I think even two parties are too many."

"You think you have it bad? How'd you like to be a guy named Chad trying to get people to make ballot changes? Most people laugh at me, and that's even before I tell them I'm from the Piffle Party."

He had a point. I felt for the guy.

"Are you really that committed to the Piffle Party, or does it pay better than working at Dunkin' Donuts?"

"If people don't start voting for Piffle Party candidates, there won't even be any more jobs at Dunkin' Donuts!" he sputtered. "You'll have your orders taken by some guy sitting at a computer in Bangladesh and nobody here will even have any job that pays enough to afford a single cruller at Dunkin' Donuts! That's why the country needs to understand the Piffle party platform! Nobody understands how urgent this is!"

"Take a deep breath, Chad," I said. Why did I feel that I was working a suicide prevention hot line?

Just to make the guy feel better, I perused the Piffle party

Web site, which informed me that some of the greatest cultural icons of America would begin a mass exodus unless the Piffle candidate became the next president. It was a sobering thought that we might lose the likes of John Mellencamp, the Dixie Chicks and Death Cab for Cutie, but I suppose it was the price of democracy.

Then I got smart. I no longer picked up the phone for any number I didn't recognize on caller ID. It was the only way I could preserve my own civil rights to try to get some work done—at least until after the election.

Reading This Warning Label May Kill You

As a society, we are grappling with some of the thorniest issues in recent memory: Should we stay the course in Iraq or go home? Should we legalize same-sex marriage? Should the government outlaw dodge ball to avoid the possibility of any child being left behind on the schoolyard with a bruised ego?

These are weighty debates that may change the face of our civilization. And yet, I am even more worried about the fact that Americans cannot buy a pair of shoes without being warned not to eat the tiny white envelope, or "PillowPak," inside the shoe. Just think about it: Has anyone really opened a box of new shoes, found the "PillowPak" inside, and said, "I was just in the mood for an envelope of odor- and humidity-absorbing ground clay!" Besides, if the manufacturers of these "PillowPaks," which are also found in purses, vitamin bottles and other products, think we are that stupid, why do they also print the warning in French and Chinese? Let's face it, anyone who is that many cans short of a six-pack and thinks that an itty-bitty package of ground clay is a snack is unlikely to have also learned to read Chinese. French, maybe, but not Chinese.

Everyone should shudder in fear about the future of a society in which manufacturers feel obliged to warn us, in type as big as my hubcaps, "DO NOT DRIVE VEHICLE WHILE THIS

HUMUNGOUS PIECE OF CARDBOARD IS ON YOUR CAR WINDSHIELD!" and "DO NOT USE WHILE SLEEPING" on labels affixed to hair dryers. If we need instructions like this, we are clearly too blunderheaded to figure out answers to the major geopolitical and social questions facing us.

We all know whom we have to thank for all this great spilling of ink: trial lawyers. It only took one ape head out of ten million people who was curious about what might happen if he drank some paint thinner to ensure that the rest of us would be tortured with inane warning labels on everything we buy. Wait, that's not true: The ape head was also helped by the doddering old fool tearing down the highway with a cup of piping hot coffee between her legs to make the rest of us have to read stickers found on toilets at public facilities that actually warn: "RECYCLED FLUSH WATER UNSAFE FOR DRINKING." Hadn't she ever heard of cup holders?

But if manufacturers think we are such dimwits, why are the warning labels on other products, such as medicines, so sophisticated that one needs a Ph.D. in chemistry to understand them? My migraine medication comes with a little booklet loaded with a whole dissertation's worth of warnings, which begin with the scary sub-heading: "Risk of Myocardial Ischemia and/or Infarction and Other Adverse Cardiac Events." My guess is that when they discuss various "cardiac events" they are not talking about running the Boston Marathon. They are telling us that while the little pill may get rid of our miserable migraine, in the process we may end up with every possible type of heart ailment contrived in a lab rat. Take it from me: You can read warning labels all day long, but just know that the bottom line of nearly every one of them contains the sobering news that in rare cases, everything—even bottled water—can kill you.

I have a theory that all these mixed messages on warning labels may be a conspiracy hatched by our enemies to weaken our resolve to fight for our freedom, or at least for the return of super-size fries at McDonalds. After all, if they can make us feel so beef-headed that we need to be told, "REMOVE CHILD FROM STROLLER BEFORE FOLDING," they will know that our self-esteem has been so seriously compromised that we won't be able to figure out whether the United Nations is our friend or not, or whether drinking 48-ounce schooners of Pepsi should be sold legally without a congressional mandate.

It's not as if I didn't have enough to do already without having to battle the warning label industry, but I can't just stand by as our nation is continually dumbed-down, one warning label at a time. I'm going to write to my congressperson right now to make my views known on the matter.

In the meantime, remember, NEVER IRON CLOTHES WHILE THEY ARE BEING WORN.

Part V:

Guys Do the Darndest Things

This Could Be You!

On any normal day, our incoming mail is predictable and boring: bills, junk advertisements, credit card come-ons, and coupons for steam cleaning my carpet. That's why I was captivated immediately by the glossy color brochure with a vivid photograph of a bunch of guys in a raft, navigating frothy white water rapids. Their eyes were bugged out and mouths agape in that distinctive combination of terror and joy that men find so irresistible. Below the photo was this teaser, all in giant capital letters:

THIS COULD BE YOU!

But of course, this couldn't be me, because this rafting deal was designed as a male-bonding thing, organized by guys, for guys. I showed the brochure to my husband when he came home. I hadn't seen him with an expression of that much terror and joy since the time he tried to teach me to ski and we narrowly missed that big tree.

"This could be you," I said, handing him the brochure. "Why don't you consider it?"

Space was limited, so before he could think of an objection, I signed him up for a two-day adventure amid burly pines, raging waters and no bathroom facilities.

But soon I had buyer's remorse. While my husband went out shopping for a wet suit, water-safe shoes and insect repellent, I read the thick packet of warnings and disclaimers that the trip organizers had sent. "There are significant risks to whitewater rafting, and previous rafting experience is strongly recommended. You could be swept overboard. Rafts, dories and kayaks do capsize, especially on the infamous Slaughter's Sluice, with its crashing eight-foot drops. Every reasonable attempt will be made to rescue rafters tossed overboard, except in cases where rafters refused requests to stop singing 'Hotel California' during the previous night's cookout."

"Maybe this wasn't such a good idea," I said to my husband. "You've never rafted in anything more dangerous than a motorboat in Marina del Rey." This was a fatally stupid thing to say to a guy. I meant no affront to his manliness. I just didn't want to end up a river rafting widow.

"I'll be fine," he huffed, packing his flashlight, sun visor and new, quick-drying pants that he bought at an outdoor adventure equipment store. "Besides, if anything happens, my life insurance is paid up."

The next day at the crack of dawn, I drove him to the airport. I kissed him goodbye and wished him a safe journey. I thought about him during the day and hoped that he wouldn't find himself somewhere on that river without his paddle. Late that night, I reached him on his cell.

"How was it?" I asked.

He tried to tell me, but words failed him, in part because he was so deliriously happy from the adrenalin rush and the male bonding, and partly because he sounded kind of sloshed. He said something about having been tossed out of the boat, which was frightening yet thrilling, but his mates had saved him. As he spoke, I heard manly shouts and laughter in the background. "I have to go now," he said. "We're about to sing 'Hotel California' again and they need me on back-up vocals."

"I guess this means you don't miss me," I said, slightly wounded.

"Nah, not really. I'm coming, guys!" He hung up.

The next evening, my husband came home a changed man. At the airport, he hugged his fellow rafters goodbye as if they had raised the flags at Iwo Jima together. Two days earlier, they had been strangers. Now, they were a band of rafting brothers, closer than any men could be. This was the natural result of having shared one boat, one tent, several rescues of guys thrown overboard on perilous Class 4 rapids, several steaks and God knows how many bottles of Scotch.

Since the trip, our friends (those we have left) have been treated to the digital slide show of my husband's rafting trip many times. "There I am, about to get tossed out of the boat!" "There we are, pitching our tents!" "Look at the other boat capsizing!" There were many photos of guys with burly arms in wetsuits, wearing helmets and cocky expressions, photos of guys resting on craggy rocks, and photos of guys eating a lot of meat.

My husband enjoyed his rafting adventure so much that he has taken to wearing his quick-dry adventure clothing around the house, perhaps in the hope that a raft will stop on our porch and some guys will shout, "C'mon in!" If they do, he'll be ready.

Naturally, I have felt left out. I've looked far and wide for a thrilling outdoor adventure for me, but nothing seems right. Dog sledding in Minnesota? Too remote. Rock climbing on some crazy, sheer cliff? You've got to be kidding. I want an adventure, but I don't have a death wish. Backpacking in the Appalachians might work if I could get my chiropractor to come along. Canoeing in mangrove tunnels sounded good until I learned that the canoeing was in Florida. Too many alligators.

Finally, I found just the thing: I'm going to Sea World with the family and will go on every ride that requires guests to be more than forty-two inches tall. This will include a ride that makes you feel like you're on a rocky helicopter ride while just sitting in a seat and a water ride that will plunge me through an underground cavern, with my seat belt securely fastened. My husband is not the only one capable of fearless exploits, you know.

Next summer, I don't plan to stand idly by while he rushes down the rapids. I, too, am entitled to some exhilaration. So far I'm debating between the Iowa State Fair and the National Spelling Bee, though the Zucchini Festival in Ludlow, Vermont is also tempting. Either way, I'll make sure to have lots of photos to show to one and all upon my return.

Please Marry Me, Darling: I Wore These Tights Just for You

Even before the nation's most emotive Scientologist, Tom Cruise, proposed very publicly to his wife, Tomkat, at the Eiffel Tower, men with romance coursing through their veins have been scheming to devise dramatic ways to propose in public. It sounds achingly romantic, but I say it's a dangerous trend that must be stopped.

First, some of these proposals are a downright menace to public safety. What could be more reckless than renting a huge billboard off the Interstate that says, "Lucille, will you marry me? I love you, Gomer" and waiting till Lucille happens to drive down that patch of the road? Maybe at just that moment when Lucille is destined to drive by that billboard she is fuming about their lengthy courtship, currently eleven years, eight months, ten days and twenty-six minutes? (Not that she's counting.) How does Gomer know that she wasn't busy writing a "Dear Gomer" e-mail in her head for his stubborn refusal to discuss the big "M"? Not only is the billboard approach cowardly (is he not man enough to say it in person?), but poor Lucille could be so shocked by the declaration that she might slam into the side of the road. Trust me: No bride wants to hobble down the aisle wearing a clunky leg cast.

Other alpha males, or alpha male wannabes, have similarly become swept up in this trend. They are snapping up books on romantic proposals and scouring the Internet for inventive ways to pop the question. As a result, we have men falling on bended knees at the pyramids in Egypt, on gondolas in Venice, and in five-star restaurants frequented by the glitterati, where the men propose loudly enough for the entire restaurant to break into wild applause as a dozen diners record the event on their cell phone-camcorders. Even bowling alleys have become soft targets for the mushy-hearted. More than one woman has had the mixed blessing of having her man propose before the rest of the teary-eyed league, while she is teased into finding her own ring somewhere in the rack of sixty-eight bowling balls behind her. All this sudden knee-dropping may be good for the chiropractic industry, but I'm not so sure it's good for women.

Women are so stunned by these public proposals that they are shocked into squealing "YES!" in front of the assembled masses, whether they want to marry the guy or not. With so many eyes on them, the couple then hug with the intensity of giant mutant squids, professing their eternal bond. One woman admitted to first calling 911, assuming that her guy had collapsed because of a heart attack and not a heart overflowing. When she realized what he was really up to, she, too, squealed.

Savvy men are also boosting their chances of success by seeking "social dynamics training" offered at romance boot camps. The boot camps teach the men to avoid male behavior that women find repulsive, such as adjusting their pants with both hands, belching, and cleaning their teeth with a nail file. Foreign men learn not to ask, "How soon do I get green card?" for at least a month after the proposal. These more gallant behaviors, unexpected as they are, obviously add to the magic of the moment. Finally, the woman basks in the sensation that she has finally taught the guy a thing or two.

Don't women have enough pressure these days without having to fend off public proposals? After all, it would take a phenomenally coldhearted female to refuse a man who went to all the trouble of dressing up like an Elizabethan nobleman and commandeered a public stage to recite Shakespearian sonnets to his fair lady in the audience, culminating in a bent-knee proposal. This takes huge gumption, especially since the man is not an actor, but a junior accountant who feels self-conscious wearing tights. But what can she do? Hundreds of strangers are crying with joy at this Hallmark moment. Let's face it, even if the woman had been planning to dump Romeo she is now stuck like epoxy.

Speaking with some measure of experience, marriage is sobering enough without orchestrating televised proposals atop the Empire State Building. One wag who has tracked this trend suspects that the fifty percent divorce rate is related to the estimated fifty percent rate of public proposals. I think both statistics are suspect, but the guy is definitely on to something.

Fortunately, it didn't occur to my husband to arrange for a Jumbotron at Wrigley Field to capture us on the screen when he popped the question. Besides, he knows how I feel about all cameras making me look fat. I wouldn't have minded his dazzling me with a three-karat marquis-cut diamond ring parked in a bucket of ice in a quiet, romantic restaurant, but my mother always taught me to be practical. My husband did propose in public, though he had the good sense to wait till the smelly vagrant on the park bench next to us had rolled away first. I began to wonder why he suddenly seemed nervous, but it all became clear when he, too, bent down on one knee and handed me a proposal note, written on fine stationery, and followed it up by repeating his request with actual words.

Though this was the moment I had been dreaming of (minus the nearby vagrant), for a fleeting moment I considered asking, "Can you give me a few days?" I didn't, fearing the long-awaited offer might expire. But after tears and embraces, terror set in. At dinner, my future husband expressed his tender feelings by mumbling, "I'm sure this is a good idea, I'm sure of it," while drowning his anxiety in hops.

It was not the proposal of my dreams, but it got the job done. In the end, that's all that mattered. Besides, the tables were turned a few months later when my husband's courage about our marriage soared and mine plummeted. The day of the wedding, somebody pushed me down the aisle, which was helpful as I was not wearing my glasses and could have easily ended up in the ladies' lounge instead of on the dais.

Happily, we've had several romantic dinners since that less-than-sentimental evening of the proposal many years ago. And I take comfort knowing that other men I had dated might have contrived far more romantic proposals, but would have made lousy husbands. Clearly, I got a far better deal. Of course it's sweet that men will arrange for Mrs. Claus to step out of a Christmas parade and propose to a young woman on behalf of a man swooning in love. But a word of warning, gentlemen: Once you pull a stunt like that, you have set the bar for romance permanently high for the rest of your marriages. Once you spring for five dozen long-stemmed red roses on Valentine's Day and light up a room with forty-seven multicolored tapers, don't expect to get away with bringing home flowers from the gas station ever again.

So women, beware: America's men are contriving to make you swoon with their public displays of affection. If you're a woman with a boyfriend and see a Jumbotron headed your way at the ball game, make a break for it, or before you can say "Strike!" you'll find yourself engaged in front of 40,000 people, with no visible means of escape.

Consider yourselves warned.

What's a Nice Guy Like You Doing in a Place Like This?

We were innocently selecting weed-killer at Home Depot when my husband asked me, "Do you think our marriage has gotten a little boring?"

"I don't know how you can say that," I said while putting a bottle of "Wild Weed Wacker" in the cart. "Wasn't it romantic last night, when we cozied up together and selected paint chips for the guest bathroom?"

"Look," he said, "today is our anniversary. Why are we spending it here? I think it's time to jazz things up." He suddenly yanked me to the side of the aisle to avoid my being run over by a tooting forklift speeding our way. Who said chivalry was dead?

"Well, let's start by not discussing the state of our marriage in the garden department of Home Depot," I shouted, in order to be heard over the forklift's incessant horn. "Besides, people are trying to run us over."

But underneath my calm demeanor, I was alarmed. After all, no wife can ignore the potentially lethal remark that her husband is yearning to "jazz things up." I had to take action. The next day I headed to the bookstore and pulled a dozen relationship books from the shelves. These ranged from the saucily titled *How to Trick Your Man into Thinking You Are Really Jennifer Lopez*, to *Mars and*

Venus in the Old-Age Home: How to Drive Each Other Wild Without Accidentally Pressing the 'Call' Button.

Wearing sunglasses to avoid detection, I hunkered down at a table to update my romance skills. In "Fear of Flirting," I took a quiz to assess my "flirtation style." Was I more like Mae West ("sassy and bold"), or Ingrid Bergman ("smooth and intriguing")? Zsa Zsa Gabor ("the accent that launched a thousand divorces") or Cher ("exotic and creative")? Sadly, my romantic style most closely matched that of Margaret Thatcher ("unabashedly free-market and proud of it"). My husband was right!

One relationship expert proposed installing camcorders throughout the house so that my husband could enjoy watching me during the day whenever he liked. I'd be his very own sexy Webcam girl! But if the sight of me cleaning lint from the dryer or fishing a plastic bottle cap out of the garbage disposal could send *frissons* of excitement through my husband, we had deeper problems than just my Margaret Thatcher mode of flirting. Besides, department stores, banks and major traffic intersections have already got cameras trained on me. Couldn't I have a little privacy in my own home?

When my husband arrived home that evening, I popped a CD of Joe Cocker's "You Are So Beautiful" on the stereo, flung my arms around him and said, "Darling, fly me to Barcelona on the Concorde!" I batted my eyelashes at him.

"Allergies bothering you again?" he asked, setting down his briefcase and sifting through the mail.

I dangled my earring suggestively, focusing on my own power as an irresistible goddess. Hubby asked, "Did you remember to call the bank about that overdraft charge?" So far, my methods were not panning out. If this continued, I might have to dress up like Bo Derek in *Tarzan*. I really didn't want to have to do that.

The next day, I called my husband every hour at work to convey my love, yet after the third call I seemed to be annoying him. In a panic, I dressed up in a sexy muscle shirt and hard hat and waited for him to come home. By the time I heard the car door slam, two boys were playing Frisbee in the living room, my daughter was shouting excitedly on the phone about a friend's new and unfortunate haircut, a teenager began to blare loud "music" from his room and the dog was trying to rid himself of fleas in an unappealing way. Still, I pretended that nothing existed in the world expect for my love and me. I sidled over to him and said in a husky timbre, "Say, what's a nice guy like you doing in a place like this?"

He looked at me oddly, not even stopping to riffle through the mail. "What's with the hard hat?" he asked. And then I felt a moment of dread in my mistake: *Men* were supposed to dress in the muscle shirts and hard hats! I was supposed to have dressed in a low-cut, slinky gown! Embarrassed, I resorted to batting my eyelashes again.

"That's not a bad look for you," he concluded, and then showed me what he had just bought on his way home. It was a book on global politics by Margaret Thatcher, and he was excited to read it. I put my arms around him and said, "Honey, I'll read you the first chapter after the kids are asleep."

Mea Canine Culpa

Dear Postal Carrier:

This is not an easy letter for me to write. For starters, you try holding a pen steady in your paws when the evolutionary process has not prepared you for such things. Frankly, I'd much prefer to get my paws around a big old rawhide bone just about now and tear it apart with my sharp, eager teeth. But learning to wield a pen is a mere physical challenge, which I, a distinguished and brilliant Beagle/Lab mix, can easily rise above.

The harder—dare I say—more repulsive aspect of this is that I resent having to apologize for barking maniacally, frothing at the mouth, and trying to kill you every day when you open the gate to deliver the mail. As a dog, this is my official duty. I have heard some friends of my Human Companion (as a minority yourself, you can well understand why I don't use the odious word "owner" to explain our relationship) laugh that my behavior fits the stereotype of the dog who hates the mailman. Well, I ask you, where do stereotypes come from if not real-world examples that are repeated ad nauseum?

Anyway, my HC has told me that you have threatened to stop delivering mail altogether unless I am "controlled." That would be just fine by me. As far as I can see, all you bring are bills, bills, more bills, and solicitations for Thai restaurants and contracting services that this family has no use for. When's the last time you delivered a thoughtful, handwritten thank-you note? An unexpected birthday check from a distant aunt? Think about it.

This used to be a classy neighborhood, before it was infested with undesirables, like that ugly pair of Boxers down the block and the Rottweiler only three doors away. But I know that even those lower forms of canine will not just sit quietly when they can smell you coming down the block, carrying that sack of good-for-nothing bulk mail envelopes. If they didn't act to protect their turf, they'd hardly deserve the proud name of "dog."

And you of all people, working for the United States Postal Service, ought to appreciate the increasing need for vigilance in security matters. Some people wait for that bozo at the Department of Homeland Security to announce his new scary color of the week (this week's is aubergine, if I'm not mistaken) before deciding how hysterical to get regarding potential terror threats. But as so many others have learned through painful experience, I can't afford to wait for the government to act before going on high alert. In this house, I *am* the Department of Homeland Security, and every day is code red. I am always prepared to protect my little piece of turf against potential insurgents, terrorists, radicals, and gas company meter readers. It would be child's play to get hold of a postal carrier's uniform and hide a bomb in that sack. In a saner world, I wouldn't have to think this way, but I'd be remiss if I didn't consider all possibilities.

I admit that I did once bite you, tearing your pant leg and causing you to have twelve stitches. I regret the incident. But look at the bright side: At least my rabies shots were up to date. (FYI, I wouldn't bet on that being true for the Rottweiler.) If you got to know me in a more intimate social setting, you'd see that I am really very intelligent, sociable, loving and affectionate. That business about us being high-strung is pure rubbish, put out there by a jealous breeder of Golden Retrievers. But don't forget that I'm also a hound, used frequently for police work and narcotics detection. You bring any contraband near my gate and I'll know it before you even get past the boxers' house.

Finally, don't think I take pleasure in having my naps interrupted every day by your intrusions. You usually come right after lunch, when I'm heavy into a deep REM cycle, dreaming of successful squirrel chases, leftover steak, and my girlfriend, Maggie. You know, you non-animals are not the only ones into hybrids these days; Maggie's a Yorkie-Poo, strong-willed but with a personality that just won't quit. And you should see her coat! Silky, yet non-shedding at the same time. I met her at the dog park. She pretended not to notice me, but I know she was just being coy. I've been hinting to my HC to get me over to that dog park more often, but sometimes HCs can be a little slow on the uptake. I can't wait to show Maggie my new, red dog collar with its impressively large silver studs. Most females are simply helpless in the face of it. But why am I telling you all this? I just got carried away by my dreams of Maggie.

I'm not really sure how much *détente* you can expect between us, Mr. Postal Carrier. You have your job to do, and I respect that, but I also have mine. Don't take it personally that I hate you. I also have equal loathing for the gas meter reader, the UPS man, and the police, who showed up one day to investigate an alleged attempt on the UPS man's life. That incident was totally blown out of proportion, I assure you. Look, I don't respond well to uniforms, okay? If you could lose the uniform I think we would get along just fine.

Writing this letter has cut pretty deeply into my nap time so I'm signing off now. If you could try to arrange to bring some more friendly and personalized mail, along with some bacon-flavored dog bones, it could only help.

Woofingly,

Ken

Singing the Dodger Blues

I should have known better than to agree to go with the family to the Dodger game on Sunday. The last time I sang a rousing round of "Take Me Out to the Ball Game" with 50,000 other people the game was so unutterably boring that I swore off baseball games forever—except for Little League games featuring one of my sons on the pitching mound.

But the pressure was building. I'm married to a baseball fan and am the mother of three sports fanatics who get withdrawal shakes if they endure more than a half hour without a hit of sports gossip on the all-sports, all-the-time radio station. A torn hamstring or a flare-up of an old injury in any of the starting lineup is grist for hours of heated, on-air speculation about how long a player will languish on the disabled list. How long could I recuse myself from my family's passion for the Great American Pastime?

I realized the time had come when my sixteen-year-old son had bought a block of seats for a game and was selling tickets to many of his "closest friends"—defined as total strangers who also frequent a Dodger chat room. There, these "friends" devote copious amounts of time fuming at bad umpire calls in previous games. When I told him to count me in for a ticket, he was so shocked he actually unhooked his iPod from his ear to make sure he had heard right.

We had great seats above third base, and I loved the heady

smell of popcorn and the infectious enthusiasm of the fans. I marveled at the beautifully manicured field, mowed to geometric perfection. Clearly, the Dodgers had a far more competent gardening service than we had. The baseball spirit had descended on me, and even the little kid behind us lobbing peanut shells at the back of our heads did not dampen my enthusiasm—at first.

Unfortunately, it was so hot that you could have cooked a Dodger Dog on the seats. If I were to get heat stroke, I hoped at least it would be an exciting game. But when my son's Internet pals arrived, my parental radar went on high alert. In my sexist, reactionary thinking, I assumed that all his fellow baseball addicts would be, well, *fellows*. Yet most were female, young, and scantily clad. One rushed over and hugged my son. One girl had pierced her ear repeatedly until she simply ran out of cartilage. A third gal had dyed her hair in every shade of red imaginable, and a few that were unimaginable. Were these girls really experts on outfielding strategies, or were they out for another kind of score? I prepared to jump the row and plunk myself down next to my son in case any of these hussies got any funny ideas during the seventh-inning stretch. I just hoped that if the time came, the gum on the floor wouldn't stick to my shoe, preventing me from stopping an unauthorized play in the row below.

With my son as head cheerleader, we rose and gave our Los Angeles Dodgers a thunderous welcome as they ambled onto the field and began stretching and strutting. But their opponent, the Philadelphia Phillies, pitched a no-hitter until well into the sixth inning. After the Dodgers lost their pitcher to a stretched tendon, the relief pitcher stood on the mound in silent prayer, making the sign of the cross. By that time I was so miserably hot and bored that I thought about doing the same thing. And I'm Jewish.

I went down to the field level to sign up as a designated

driver, and pledged not to imbibe any alcoholic beverage during the game. I didn't want to really have to cart home any drunks, but becoming a designated driver at Dodger stadium is the only way to score a free small soft drink (a four dollar value!). Frankly, I am too cheap to spend four bucks on a small soda, and I was not surprised to see lines twenty people deep at every ATM around. With beers at seven bucks a pop, garlic fries at five dollars and fifty cents and a Super Dodger Dog for four dollars and fifty cents, you needed a favorable cash flow to chow down during the game.

By the seventh-inning stretch, several people had fallen asleep in our row, or perhaps they just had heat stroke. One of the girls in my son's group had been reduced to reading the ingredients list on her glitter lip gloss. When it was time to sing "Take Me Out to the Ball Game," I improvised some lyrics:

Take me out of this ball game,
I'd rather be at the mall.
Stop throwing your peanuts and Cracker Jack,
I'm missing a sale at the Nordstrom Rack!
I did root, and hoot for the home team,
But they're playing such a lame game.
For it's one, two, three strikes, I'm out
Of this old ball game!

My son continued to shout baseball strategy relentlessly to the players till he had completely lost his voice. Despite this, the Dodgers routinely popped foul balls, bunted badly and only managed one measly run in the entire match-up. Still, I'm proud that he was no fair-weather fan. Even when the Dodgers' loss was all but assured, my boy continued to cheer his team, even urging the rest of us to clap and sing, "Here we go Dodgers, here we go!"

Best of all, he was not distracted by all females *en désha-billé* surrounding him. He was there for one reason and one reason only: to express his unflagging, unwavering, total commitment to our home team, even when they played a pathetic game.

That made it all worthwhile.

If the Pants Still Fit, Keep It Zipped

Sometimes, even the best-trained husbands are capable of colossal judgment errors. Just last week, mine sauntered over to the dinner table sporting a haberdashing pair of elegant black slacks and snazzy shirt and tie.

"Look!" he announced. "My wedding pants still fit perfectly. Not bad after seventeen years!" Believe it or not, he twirled around.

I shook my head sadly. "We were this close to our eighteenth anniversary," I said. "Why'd you have to blow it now?" I brooded in my seat, where I wore a comfy garment ingeniously designed with an elastic waistband. It was unarguably a size larger than my wedding dress. Maybe two.

"Does your wedding dress still fit, Mommy?" our daughter asked.

"Certainly," I said. "The sleeves, anyway."

Could I actually shoehorn my body back into the wedding dress? My inquiring daughter insisted on knowing, so I was buttonholed in more ways than one.

Even as I began to unwrap the lace and polyester confection from its plastic, I could see the dress had shrunk alarmingly over the years. No doubt this was caused by oxygen deprivation. What else could I expect? It had been sealed off for nearly two decades in a zippered plastic bag, shriveling its very molecules. Really, it was a miracle there was any fabric left at all. I pulled the dress over my head and slid my arms into the armholes, but in a horrid moment of clarity, I realized that my arms, now hoisted aloft, were stuck in that position, as if I were being held up at gunpoint.

Fortunately, I discovered that some of the material was caught on a hook. I released the material, which permitted the dress to fall a few inches and rest on my hip bones. Unfortunately, this was the last outpost, where the rubbery part of me met the unforgiving textile road. Short of ripping a seam (an irresistible temptation) the dress would travel no farther. If only I had given the dress more oxygen, it never would have come to this.

A few minutes later, I cracked the door to the dining room a few inches. "Okay, now you've seen me," I whispered.

"Open the door!" my daughter demanded. "Why is the dress so short? Why are the shoulders falling off? It doesn't fit you at all."

"I don't remember the neckline being that revealing," my husband added.

"Well . . . ." I could hardly speak, since now I was the one dangerously oxygen-deprived. Still, I had managed to zip the dress up only about a quarter of the way up, creating the unintentional cascading effect of the dress neckline.

"It's much better to see the dress on video," I said, "even though as we all know the camera adds ten pounds. After dinner we'll all sit down to watch it."

"When are you coming back to serve dinner?" a son asked. He wouldn't notice if I wore an ill-fitting wedding dress, a roll of aluminum foil, or a chicken suit, as long as the hamburgers were on the table.

"Sure thing," I said, backing away from the doorway quickly and feeling a draft on my back. With relief, I slipped back into something more comfortable. Something with an elastic waistband.

Back at the table, I observed that fitting into one's wedding dress decades after the event was highly overrated and typical of the shallow values in our society. "Men can wear dress slacks to any number of occasions and look appropriate," I reasoned. "But where is a woman going to wear a ten-pound dress with pouffy sleeves other than to her own wedding? To the UPS station? The supermarket? Even if she wore a wedding dress to someone else's wedding she'd just look deranged."

"Please pass the potatoes," my husband requested. I dished out a schooner's worth of potatoes on his plate, not that it would help. His metabolism runs faster than a marathoner from Kenya; mine is slower than a camel ride across Egypt. In fact, after I'm gone I'm thinking of leaving my metabolism to the National Institutes of Health. Maybe they'll have better luck with it than I did.

My humiliating reunion with my wedding dress simply reminded me that my training of this husband is far from complete. My next lesson—given in stealth as all other lessons have been—will undoubtedly zero in on the unspoken rule that if your wedding pants still fit after seventeen years, just keep the information zipped.

Old Spice Remembers

When I was growing up, my father was always sure to get a gift on Father's Day. And I do mean "a gift": Each year, we presented him with a new bottle of Old Spice aftershave. After all, he already had season tickets to the UCLA Bruin basketball and football games. He was not on intimate terms with wrenches, pliers, or other home-repair gadgets. He didn't hunt, fish, or engage in other similar guy hobbies. The Old Spice seemed unutterably unimaginative, year in and year out, but we learned not to tinker with success.

One year we daringly ventured into uncharted gift territory and gave him a new fragrance. But Dad, who would have been a terrible poker player, could only feign pleasure. After spraying a bit on the back of his hand and then taking a whiff, he wrinkled his nose in a way that spoke volumes. All he really wanted was another bottle of Old Spice.

Dad's life wasn't easy. Born with a severe hearing deficit, he went through life struggling to catch the conversations around him. His hearing aid often whistled inconveniently (such as during movies) and could only partially compensate for his missing hearing. This handicap greatly limited his career options and his income. Many people, including, sometimes, his own family members, lacked the patience to speak slowly so that Dad could read their lips. It was a frustrating way to live. Yet sometimes, if we said things in Dad's presence that we were sure he couldn't hear, he'd whip around and say, "I heard that! I can hear when I want to!" I suppose we all hear selectively from time to time. But Dad was blessed in many ways as well. When he was twenty-one, he met my mother at a summer camp where both were counselors. Dad was a lifeguard, fit, tanned and handsome. Mom was a gorgeous sixteen-year-old who looked stunningly like Elizabeth Taylor. Naturally, Mom's parents insisted that Dad wasn't good enough for their girl, but two years later, in 1947, they walked Mom down the aisle. I still have the ceramic bride and groom that sat atop my parents' wedding cake. These days they make them out of plastic.

Nothing was more important to Dad than my mother and their children. Nothing shook his adoration or his passion for her, despite many rocky years during which family illness, financial woes, and even tragedy struck. After more than forty years of marriage, Mom, a natural brunette, lightened her hair to a burnt honey. It was beautiful. But Dad, the man who never wanted anything other than Old Spice for Father's Day, protested this change in Mom's looks.

"When I married you your hair was dark brown!" Dad argued.

"When I married you, you had hair!" retorted Mom, ending the discussion. Mom and Dad raised their children during times of enormous cultural upheaval. Like so many parents who had grown up in simpler times, they didn't like much of what was happening in society, but were powerless to stop the unwelcome changes. They also worried terribly that my brother would get drafted into the Vietnam War. As a young child, I listened to discussions around the table when my parents, aunt and grandparents tried to reassure themselves that Allan's draft number was low, decreasing his odds of being drafted. In fact, Allan didn't get called. But while driving to visit our grandmother on her birthday in March 1970, his car careened off a cliff, and he died. Life as we knew it, with its veneer of safety, ended forever that day.

Over the next many years, Dad's pain was almost unbearable to watch. Mom's pain, no less acute, remained in a deeper, closed place. Her job was to keep the family together, despite her anguish, and that's what she did. There is no such thing as "normal" life after a tragedy of this magnitude, but somehow, one puts one foot in front of the other and forges ahead. Dad's love for Mom, my sister and me continued limitlessly, but something in him died on the day that he lost his firstborn and only son. His eyes bore the pain, and even years later, he often looked a little bewildered, as if he still could not believe that this horrendous tragedy had been visited upon him.

After my husband and I married, Dad expressed concern about our rapid family expansion. We had three sons in little more than four years. Didn't we think that was enough? But when Dad was diagnosed with cancer, he had a change of heart. One day, while Mom and I sat at his bedside in the hospital, Dad shocked me by declaring that he had given the matter a lot of thought and realized how nice it would be if I had a little girl. Not only that, he already had selected names for us, including his all-time favorite girl's name, Muriel. Mom and I laughed out loud. There were precious few Muriels on the playground in the 1990s. The 1890s, probably, but not the 1990s. I remained deeply struck by Dad's talk of my having a daughter because it was so completely out of character. Although I was convinced that Dad was angry at God and had been for many years, I wondered if the Almighty was compensating Dad for his weakening physical condition with some kind of spiritual insight.

A few months later, I learned that I was expecting again. And exactly forty-eight hours later, on the Friday before Father's Day, Dad passed away. Dad's hope came true; we were blessed with a daughter. We did not name her Muriel. Instead, as is the Jewish custom, we chose to memorialize Dad with a name that began with the first letter of his Hebrew name. I'm fairly hopeful that he forgave us. Raising our children now, my husband and I share our own parents' alarm at the continued slipping away of certain bedrock values in society. To borrow a phrase from the 1960s, we feel that these changes are harmful to children and other living things. If Dad were alive today, he'd be disgusted that a TV model of fatherhood morphed from Ozzie Nelson to Ozzie Osbourne. How did this happen?

On Father's Day, after opening his aftershave, Dad loved to read his cards aloud. He read each card, even the hokey ones, with the fervor and seriousness of a Shakespearian sonnet. When I was grown, I stopped giving store-bought cards and wrote my own personal notes to Dad, trying to convey my appreciation for all his love and support over the years. Living with Dad wasn't always easy, but it was easy to forgive him for the rough patches. He faced major professional disappointments and the most painful kind of personal tragedy. How could I judge him? Of course, Dad lives on through me and my children. Funny little characteristics have wended their way through the gene pool: One of my kids loves to read his birthday cards aloud. Another has Dad's exact coloring; another, his nose. A few, I'm happy to see, share his love of people and genuine happiness at making new friends. And one of his grandsons has recently discovered a new favorite fragrance. It's called Old Spice.

Part VI:

Just Wait Till You Have Stretch Marks of Your Own

A Louse-y Plan Is Hatched

My husband and I had just landed in New York for a weekend getaway, our first in three years. After working day and night for a week to get ready for the trip, I felt heady with excitement. I had even managed to get through airport security without having to remove my shoes or surrender my tweezers. Life was good.

We were still in the car heading to the hotel when my cell phone starting thrumming in my purse. I sensed this was a bad development. The only people who call me on the cell phone are my kids, and they only call to alert me to a crisis, such as the discovery that we are out of ketchup and it's hot dog night.

I answered fearfully, the way one does when one suspects it's the principal calling again, saying it's time to reconvene to discuss young Cheyenne and her "need for excessive socialization during class."

"Hello Mommy?" It was my charming young daughter. "Bad news, Mommy. Me and the boys have lice."

Now I had contingency plans for many emergencies likely to strike during my absence, such as ear infections, civil unrest and earthquakes. But tiny disgusting insects appended to my children's heads? This was one I hadn't figured on.

"You have *lice*???" I screamed. "Are they sure?"

"Yeah. You need to pick us up. *Right now.*"

"I can't pick you up! You are in Los Angeles and I'm on the Long Island Expressway!" I was in total disbelief. Why had the good Lord done this to me? I tip fairly. I hold doors open for people. I don't even eat the last donut in the box, and don't think that's an easy thing. Where was the justice in this?

Meticulous plans for childcare and sleep-over arrangements were now down the drain. Who would take my plague-infested children now? I spent the next two hours on the phone, calling in favors (real and imagined) from friends and relatives back home. No amount of pleading, begging or groveling was beneath me. It would take a village to de-louse my children. And the villagers would have to: I was on vacation!

Talk about a bad hair day.

But that wasn't all. Because, as everyone knows, lice are equal opportunity vermin. They not only infest heads, they also infest every molecule of clothing, bedding, and teddy bears (no matter how fragile) under your roof. If you are unwilling to do 450 loads of laundry, you can simply take all the contents of your household, including the children, and have them hermetically sealed for two weeks, after which time experts claim it is safe to unseal them.

Happily, my pleading, begging and groveling worked. After knocking back a few margaritas later that evening, I basked in the comfort of knowing that I had real, true friends, the kind who buckled under the pressure of hearing my cries of desperation and, okay, threats of blackmail. I had friends who left the comfort of their own homes to come to my quarantined abode to lather up my kids with smelly anti-lousing agents and launder my every possession.

I also discovered who wasn't my friend—namely, the school's Commandant of Lice. She was the one who at first told me not to worry, she would take care of my kids till the end of the day until their carpool picked them up. She would care for my children *as if they were her very own!* I was touched that in a world that could often be so cold, I had the great good fortune to encounter a woman so filled with the milk of human kindness. Then, she presented me with a bill for 250 smackers upon my return for services rendered.

Two weeks later, yucky things were still hatching on my kids' heads, the washing machine had suffered a nervous breakdown, and we were still oiling each other's heads as if we were expecting to be anointed to the papacy. The kids were happy to check my own scalp, an exercise that elicited many gasps of "Oh my God! I didn't know you were so gray!" and "I think I see something! Oh, never mind, I think that's just rust."

We finally resorted to more drastic measures, involving one son in particular and a military crew cut. If these diabolical creatures didn't stop erupting in our hair, the rest of us would have had to do the same thing, and I might have ended up looking like Sigourney Weaver in the movie *Aliens.* Perhaps not *exactly* like her, since she's eight inches taller than I am and we have completely different faces, but once you're walking around with a shaved head, who notices the rest of you, anyway?

All this proved one thing, in my opinion. During times when many of us still fear the threat of domestic terrorism during air travel, we don't even know the half of it. The real danger may be nesting in our kids' hair.

The Plague of the School Science Fair

ast week I asked my husband if we could go out to dinner, just the two of us.

"Are you crazy?" he said. "Don't you realize the school science fair is this Thursday night?" He did not look at me when he answered, as he was intent on gluing a map of Micronesia to our son's project display board. This was a very intricate undertaking, as Micronesia comprises approximately 4,000 islands, some of them extraordinarily tiny.

Like tax season and television "sweeps" week, the school science fair is an annual plague. The day I had proposed going out to dinner, I had run around town like a maniac hunting for a place that could laminate 4,000 islands of Micronesia in a hurry, not to mention scavenging for other materials that some of our kids requested for their projects, including eye of newt. By evening, I managed to block the dreaded topic from my mind just long enough to have asked this absurd question. Of course my husband and I wouldn't have a minute to spare until we overcame the hurdle of the school science fair.

One has to wonder, how many more generations of kids are going to compare Wisk and Tide detergents in their ability to get pomegranate stains out from a white school shirt? How many more houseplants must suffer as kids lock them in a dark closet for a week, only to discover the plants are screaming in plant language, "Let there be light!" How many times must I as a parent relive the annual bad dream that is science fair?

I pondered these weighty issues while my husband slaved away on the display board, showing the fascinating weather patterns over Micronesia. In case you are curious, these range from "balmy" to "really sunny." All this on behalf of a child who was too busy reading Harry Potter in the bathroom to come out and help. Meanwhile, I was negotiating with another son over his ideas for his own project. His ideas were strikingly original, and like any good scientist, he had performed each experiment many times to verify the results.

Despite his enthusiasm, I tried to talk him out of an experiment called, "How Long Can You Not Brush Your Teeth Before Your Gums Bleed All Over Your Shirt?" (based on his most recent visits to the dentist); "How Long Can the Hamster Spin on His Wheel While on a Calorie-Restricted Diet?," an accidental experiment with tragic conclusions; "How Long Can Old Cream Cheese Sandwiches Live Behind the Bed Before the Mold Seeps Throughout the House, Thus Requiring Major Renovations Requiring Permits?," and his personal favorite, "Which Jokes Are Most Likely to Make My Brother Laugh so Hard at the Dinner Table that Water Spurts Out His Nose?" For this one, he had even made a bar graph showing differing results based on knock-knock jokes, jokes taken from Popsicle sticks, dumb blonde jokes and Marx Brothers routines.

One might hypothesize that these ideas were of only questionable benefit to the World of Science. However, they did capture my son's imagination and spark his interest in further home-based experimentation. When we had reached a deadlock, I coerced him into doing a less personally revealing experiment. This project,

"Will Baseballs Still Bounce after Being Boiled for Nine Hours?" was taken from a real book in the library. I kept my son's baseball on a low boil in my hot water urn all day. After hours of anticipation, my son and I discovered two things. First, you will ruin your baseball after boiling it for nine hours. Second, you will also ruin your hot water urn, since it now smells permanently of baseball. (Perhaps I could try dabbing a little Wisk or Tide detergent into it, to see if I could recapture that fresh, non-baseball scent.) Utterly dismayed by these boring results, my son forged ahead with his bar graph, charting the most effective jokes to induce hilarity-based nasal sprays at the dinner table. The science fair judges awarded him first place for originality. I hope my husband gets over the disappointment soon.

If You Play This Game,
Go Directly to Jail

In an admirable effort to release American families from captivity in front of their big-screen TVs, game manufacturers have encouraged parents to institute family game night at least once a week.

In theory, this is a great idea. Games should be fun, and most anything that lures kids away from a computer or TV screen must hold some promise. But why must these games take so long? I confess that when my kids ask me to play Monopoly, I feel a sense of dread. Sure, it would be fun to secure the title to highbrow properties like Reading Railroad and Park Place, but our bouts with Monopoly often threaten to last longer than the World Series. Eventually, I feel like I need a "Get Out of Jail Free" card.

It isn't always the game's fault. My kids have an uncanny knack for developing any and all opportunities for dispute with their siblings. This can add days, weeks, and even months to the length of the average Monopoly game. I can live with the opening salvo—a fifteen-minute argument about who gets to be the cannon, who the ship, and who the hat. (Nobody ever wants to be the iron or the thimble, both symbols of the kind of domestic labor considered unfashionable under this roof.) I can also survive another twenty minutes while they argue over who is uniquely qualified to be banker. To make things simple, I recuse myself from consideration for this post and go to the kitchen to make lunches for the next day until negotiations have sputtered to a close.

But I despair when the fights break out about whether one player really had passed "Go" and collects $200 because another player insisted she had advanced only from North Carolina Avenue and not from Pacific Avenue. Other small progressions in the game that in a saner world would move without incident prove surprisingly volatile: Should rent really be doubled on Baltic and Mediterranean Avenues if another player questions whether improvements to the property had been verifiably made? Should a brother be forced to roll the dice again since one die landed outside the board, but in doing so allowed him to end up on Community Chest, yielding a $100 bounty for the maturation of a life insurance policy?

For a game that was created and trademarked in 1935, Monopoly remains remarkably up-to-date. It may not foster familial love and a case of the warm fuzzies among its players, but as the game requires a team of litigators standing by for every move on the board, it is excellent preparation for life itself.

During the interminable fourth hour of our last round of Monopoly, nerves became frayed over the true ownership of the Short Line Railroad. Demands were shouted to either prove ownership or concede the game, and I listlessly reminded my kids that playing Monopoly was supposed to be fun. However, I could not be heard above their yelling, so I went into the bathroom and watched seventeen more hairs turn gray. When I heard the neighbors slam the windows shut and a police helicopter hover overhead, I had no choice but to terminate fun family game night.

Thankfully, it has been six months since anyone has tried to play Monopoly around here. (It may have something to do with that noise complaint we received from the Police Department.) Even better, we have moved onto quieter, shorter games. One of our new favorites is Boggle, which challenges players to find words in a grid of jumbled letters. Best of all, each round only lasts three minutes. This ensures that when you sit down to play, you probably won't still be there when your next birthday rolls around.

Boggle can also be surprisingly educational. For example, last week I played with my three sons late at night. After the first round was finished, my sixteen-year-old read his list of words first.

"I've got 'lust,'" he said, and I realized that if anyone were to find this word in Boggle, it would be a sixteen-year-old boy.

"Me too," added the fourteen-year-old.

"I've got 'lust' too," my twelve-year-old piped up in his still improbably high voice. Their tone was nonchalant, as if only someone playing blindfolded could have missed it. But I had missed it, along with other words that had fairly leaped out at my sons: sex, gas, leggy, base, ball, and gore.

Here were the words that I found: sag, dye, slut, sale, roast, and sore. I suggested that we play again so I could mine the further psychological dimensions of my boys while still going in for the kill. This, to me, was a clear win-win. Unlike Backgammon, where I am no longer certain to beat the kids, I am—for the moment—fairly certain to lick them in Boggle. I never went in for that namby-pamby parenting advice about letting your kids beat you in a game once they're over eight or nine. After that, it's every player for himself or herself.

I am thankful that Monopoly has lost its appeal, as I was on the verge of dumping family game night for good. True, I never realized my dream of building a hotel on Boardwalk, but I have made peace with it. Besides, we are all enjoying our new game challenges even more, despite the lack of open hostilities among siblings. The other day, I spied my twelve-year-old studying a dog-eared copy of

Backgammon for Blood in brow-furrowed concentration. I smiled as I watched him. I'll be happy when he finally beats me, and he will feel like a worthy opponent. Maybe, just maybe, our days of having the neighbors slam their windows shut on our family game nights are finally over.

The Motherboard Has Blown

I was puzzling over the age-old problem of how to deal with children who fail to listen to me when my computer did me a big favor and issued a failure message on the screen. This offered me an unexpected parenting epiphany: Maybe I needed to talk to my kids as if I were the computer! After all, when the computer tells them to do something, they snap to it.

When the kids trooped in after school, dumping their sweaty socks and backpacks on the floor, I said, "To decrease risk of being infected with a virus, remove sweaty socks and replace with dry ones before you shut down."

They looked at me askance, yet still left their socks on the living room floor.

"Error extracting sweaty socks," I said. "Insert socks into laundry drive. Reboot."

"What's wrong with you, Mom?" asked one son. "And what's for dinner?"

"Mother has insufficient memory. Do you want to save recovered leftovers from the other night's meatloaf as RESCUE. DINNER.EAT?"

"Leftovers are gross," opined a youngster. "Can't you make something fresh?"

"Bad command, bordering on insubordination. Press 'Normal Wash' key on the dishwasher, and remember to add soap. Otherwise you will lose any unsaved allowance for the rest of the week. Press 'Permanent Press' button on the dryer to restart your mother."

"Can I have the car tonight?" my eldest asked.

"Access denied. Invalid signature attribute." I wasn't even sure what that last sentence meant, but it sounded authentic.

"Why not? I don't have homework," he prodded.

"To regain access, delete the trash folder piling up in your room. Click OK if you swear you will drive using SAFE MODE. Upload clean dishes from dishwasher onto shelves and in cutlery drawer. Click YES or NO to continue."

"Okay, we get the point," my daughter said. "What's for dinner? We're hungry."

Suddenly my plan didn't seem like such a hot idea. Only three minutes into the scheme and I was running out of error commands. Still, if computers could repeat the same error message over and over, why couldn't I?

"Mother has encountered a fatal execution error in children demanding new cuisine daily. Do you want to save recovered leftovers from the other night's meatloaf as RESCUE.DINNER.EAT or do you want to go hungry? Warning: Do not use curser in my presence."

"Mom, knock it off!"

"To print out error log, click OK," I said. "You are also bugging your mother. Do you wish to debug? If so, sweep the kitchen and take dog for walk."

"Uh, Mom? Mrs. Winston may call from the school to tell you about something that happened in class, but I didn't do it," a boy confessed.

"Your mother has become unstable and may shut down. Collect overdue library books from around the house and then click OK."

I heard a collective groan from my frustrated children. Finally, they had a taste of what it felt like to be ignored!

"Seems like Mom is suffering from insufficient disk space," one of the kids diagnosed.

"Could be an invalid switch, or a general protection fault. Should we call somebody?"

This was amazing. When I am truly sick, these kids are completely oblivious, but when I sound like a FAQ page from Microsoft, they're worried.

Before I knew it, Mr. Computer Doctor, otherwise known as Hank, made a house call. He was equipped with tool kit and back-up CDs in case I lost any remaining memory during the repair session.

"We've tried to reboot Mom repeatedly but she's still malfunctioning. She also can't seem to read any normal file directories," my eldest told him. "Think you can help?"

"We can try to download a repair patch, but if her entire motherboard is shot, you have no choice but to get a whole new parent," Hank said. He put a stethoscope to my chest and asked me to breathe deeply. He recommended a major upgrade for me, as well as a visit to a psychiatrist.

"Okay, the jig is up," I told everybody. "I just wanted to see what it would take to get your attention, but I can't afford to keep it at Hank's hourly rate. But as long as you're here, why not double-check the smut filters on the computers? Meanwhile, I guess I'll go make dinner."

The kids high-fived one another. My attempt at creative parenting had morphed into a computer upgrade for the kids, while I was left as the short-order cook—again.

Turning the Pages of Childhood

"**M**ommy, will you read to me?"

My ten-year-old daughter asks me this question every night. Even if I'm exhausted, or just want some time to myself, I almost always say yes. Before I turn around, she'll be eleven, then twelve, then a teenager. She will no longer need her "reading fix" with Mommy.

"Time will not be ours forever," as Ben Jonson wrote back in 1607, when the printed word was still a new invention. I want to make this time with my daughter last.

My husband and I also have three sons, older than Yael, so I have clocked fifteen solid years of reading aloud to our children. Because we have worked to instill a love for books in our children, Yael's requests for me to read to her make me feel that we have succeeded.

I take special delight in being asked to read to a child who is a veteran independent reader, and her brothers all did the same thing. Over the years, we have enjoyed countless delicious reading experiences together: Roald Dahl's magical *Charlie and the Chocolate Factory*, E.B. White's timelessly charming *Charlotte's Web*, Beverly Cleary's series about the irrepressible Ramona and Henry Huggins, and so many more.

I missed this kind of quiet entertainment growing up. Memories of my childhood are filled with the theme song to *Bonanza* bouncing out from one bedroom where my father watched, competing with the canned laugh track of *The Odd Couple* in the den, where my Mom and I watched. We watched others live imaginary lives more than we talked about our own real ones, substituting passive entertainment for active engagement with one another. For this reason, I find the time I spend reading with my children particularly sweet and poignant.

I once fancied myself an aspiring actress, and had a few years of training in theatre arts. Now my performances are pretty much limited to the dramatic readings I do from *Ramona the Pest* or *Runaway Ralph*. That's fine with me. My audience may be small, but they're enthusiastic and appreciative. And in addition to having fun, I'm also learning right along with them. Over the years and through the pages, I learned that Mickey Mantle was the most powerful switch-hitter in baseball history, that Haym Solomon, a Polish-born Jew, was responsible for raising most of the money to finance the American Revolution, and that Helen Keller, despite being sightless and deaf, graduated *cum laude* from Radcliffe.

My husband and I may have fostered our kids' love of the written word by our reading to them when they were small, but as they grew, they made this gift their own. It will surely enhance their lives for as long as God grants them time on this Earth.

When our kids are all grown up, I hope that their memories of our reading together, snuggling on the couch or in bed, will be among the most meaningful of their childhoods. I know that they already are for me.

Moms Go Hollywood, Then Go Home

My friend Liz called me up and out of the clear blue sky invited me to go with her and our friend Leslie to a club.

"Sam's Club or Wal-Mart?" I asked.

"You've been housebound way too long," Liz said. "A club with a band and dancing. You know, the kind where we used to go for fun!"

After so many years of motherhood, I had completely forgotten that music clubs even existed, or that I might one day enter them again. Before giving Liz an answer, I quickly made some calculations:

I could decline, enabling me to make dinner for the family, keep my promise to one of my kids to who was struggling with an essay on how we must all do our part to save the snail darter from extinction, and tackle that mountain of laundry that I'd been assiduously avoiding for five days. Or I could accept, leaving my husband to cope with all of the above.

"What time do we leave?" I asked, nearly swooning from the frothy feeling of spontaneity.

I dashed to my closet, but no black leather pants or other couture appropriate for a Sunset Boulevard hangout suddenly sprouted from the hangers. Most of my clothing shouted "Parent-Teacher Conference Night" more than "House of Blues." I had only twenty minutes, and half of that time was devoted to scrubbing whole wheat bread dough from my fingernails and picking dog hair off a black pullover sweater.

Liz and Leslie were knocking at the door just as my husband arrived from work. I waved and blew a kiss as I brushed past him.

"Where's Mom going?" he asked the kids.

"She's going clubbing in Hollywood. Said she'd be back by Wednesday," one of them answered. "Do you think she's starting a mid-life crisis?"

We were almost at the club when it occurred to me to ask whom we were going to hear. As if it mattered! Liz said it was a Scottish band, so I conjured visions of bagpipes and guys in kilts. This can be a good look for some men, though Prince Charles is better off with his knees covered if you ask me. Besides, my plumber is Scottish, and I love his accent. As long as the band didn't sing about copper pipes or say things like "Great mother of Jesus, would you look at this!" I'd be happy.

It had been a long time since I'd been to a club other than the Sam's Club variety, and it seemed to me that clubs had gotten darker, louder, and more security-conscious since I last visited one.

After our handbags were riffled through, we were semi-frisked, slapped with plastic bracelets and given access to the opening band, "Nuclear Stubble," which was enthusiastically smashing all our Eustachian tubes and the ganglia attached to our brains. They were louder than a nuclear detonation, though not quite as musical. My intestines were doing cartwheels, my heart threatening to catapult through my bra (despite its having underwire support) and out of my chest. Liz, Leslie and I all covered our ears. Suddenly, our fun girls' night out threatened to look like a long evening. The club's "No in-and-out" policy ensured we were caged inside until our Scots took stage. I was sure I'd be deaf as a post by then.

As we stood huddled with our ears covered, a beefy, brawny, bald bruiser swaggered over to us. Were those very large rings on every one of his fingers, or brass knuckles? Either way, whatever he came over to say, I'd agree, especially if he asked us to leave the club. Maybe he thought that the appearance of a trio of bourgeoisie minivan moms like us might give the club a bad rap.

Without a word, he handed us each tiny plastic bags containing neon orange foam ear plugs. We joyfully ripped the packages open, but even with the plugs in, Nuclear Stubble still sounded like a nuclear blast, only under water.

"This is fun!" yelled Liz.

"WHOSE NEW SON?" I asked. I never excelled at lip reading.

"THIS . . . IS . . . FUN!" she screamed. Leslie and I nodded in agreement, and my left ear plug popped out. We all dove to the floor to search for it. Now not only did we look like a bunch of minivan moms who made a wrong turn on the way to the bake sale, we had neon orange foam buttons jutting out from our ears. Liz had been right about one thing: The show *was* standing room only, because the place had no chairs, except for one tiny area where bar stools were roped off. Mr. Brass Knuckles indicated those seats were for "special members" of the club, but after Liz palmed a $20 bill on him, he had a change of heart.

Eventually, Nuclear Stubble ended their "performance," and my heart began to recover. We viewed quick promo videos of upcoming shows at the club, including such musical luminaries as Poisoned Meade, DethGrip, and Strangled Sausage.

The Scottish band did not wear kilts. Nor did they play

bagpipes. They were a good old rock and roll band, and one of the lead singers even looked like my high school math teacher. They were in every way superior to Nuclear Stubble, and did not seem intent on deafening the audience. Though to be honest, some couples in the audience wouldn't have cared, as they had mistaken the dance floor for a bedroom—an understandable mistake, given the similar features of having hundreds of people, strobe lights, and a live seven-piece band in the same room. A peppy group of guys who looked like advisors to the show *Queer Eye for the Straight Guy* also distracted me. I couldn't help but wonder how they got their shirts pressed to perfection like that. But I was too shy to ask.

After the show, we agreed it was way too late to go out for coffee, nearly eleven o'clock! Carpool beckoned us all early the next day. This also differed from our younger, more hedonistic days when we would have continued the party till the wee hours of the morning.

Next week the three of us are going to try another club. After all, who can resist such a great deal on heated mattress pads and garage floor protectors?

Letters to Camp Cashorchecka

I sat down to write a letter to my boys who are away at camp, and after my fingers flew across the keyboard, this is what emerged:

Dear Boys:

Have you been gone for a week already? Time sure is flying by! I'm finally getting the hang of cooking for just Dad, your sister and me. Now I realize how much chow you guys can pack away! I never knew a chicken could last through two meals, or that it might take three days to fill the dishwasher, instead of every four hours when you're all home. The house is nice and tidy since you are not dropping sweaty socks everywhere, and I am feeling oh so relaxed since I am not standing over the computer, trying to peel you off it every night. However, I admit that a few times Dad has had to haul me off the computer! With so much less laundry to do, I've found so many fun things to do online and am now positively addicted to a word game called Text Twist. I guess I have a little more sympathy for you and your own computer game compulsions now but we will still have to implement some new rules about computer time when you get back, especially since you'll have to share the machine with me, too.

When I am not playing Text Twist (or Internet Backgammon with people in Belgium), Dad and I are having a blast. Since your sister goes to sleep at 8:00 p.m., and we aren't spending all night chasing the rest of you to bed, we are enjoying the novel sensation of having evenings to ourselves. Did I mention we got a new DVD player? We're watching a whole slew of movies we have wanted to see for ages and that are thematically inappropriate for you, but hey, why shouldn't we have a little vacation, too? Last night we had Italian food delivered and ate out in the gazebo and drank a bottle of wine. I never knew sending you to summer camp could be so much fun!

I'm sorry to hear that you feel that some of your bunkmates are not taking enough Ritalin. Perhaps you can discuss this with the camp director. I am happy, though, that you missed spearing your senior counselor during archery lessons. You are right that few people carry enough liability insurance to cover that kind of injury.

Are you remembering to brush your teeth? Please don't come back looking like Fifteenth Century barn hands. Don't lose your retainers, either. We are already deducting the cost of each lost retainer from your college funds, and we're nearly talking community college, okay? Must run now. Your sister's stashed away at a friend's house and Dad and I are off for a dinner picnic at the beach.

Love you!
Mom

I reread the letter, looking for any grammatical or spelling errors, which would obviously set a bad example. Yet, somehow, while the spelling was okay, the letter didn't seem to strike the appropriate note of maternal longing. I wrote a new letter.

Dear Boys:

We miss you so much! Each time we sit down to dinner, your empty chairs and the mounting leftovers (it's so hard to adjust to cooking for only three) remind me that you are thousands of miles away. I am happy you are having fun, or at least I assume you are having fun, since you only called once. (And please remember that when you call us after breakfast where you are, it is still only 5:30 in the morning here, okay?) When I did reach you the other day at a more respectable hour and you didn't recognize my voice, it made me sad. Please use the enclosed phone card to call us at least once a week (after 5:30 a.m.!) so you don't forget the sound of my voice. I've enclosed a photo as well so you will remember what I look like.

Things are pretty dull around here without you. Dad and I have a little more free time in the evenings now, so the other night Dad decided to check the smoke detector batteries before they all started chirping in the middle of the night. Good thing I had written that task on the calendar so we wouldn't forget! I also got the smog check for the car and sent in for the new registration, and today I plan to wipe down the baseboards around the house. How's that for excitement? I took the dog for his rabies and distemper shots, and the vet said he looked healthy but he needs to have his teeth brushed more often. I can't quite picture Ken doing this on his own, so you know what that means: One more job for me! Sometimes we are so lonely without you here that the only thing we can think of to do is play Frisbee with Ken, but that gets old pretty fast, at least for us.

Speaking of brushing teeth, please don't neglect this important part of your daily routine. Cavities are really expensive, you know. Maybe I should not have sent you those home-baked chocolate chip cookies but I wanted you to have something special from me on Visitor's Day since we live too far from camp to have made the trip. (I hope you got those cookies by now; I sent them Priority Mail so they would still be fresh.)

Oh, remember those library books you swore up and down we had returned but that the library insisted that we had not? I found them under the bunk beds. Unfortunately, they were pretty badly mutilated, and anyway the late fees were higher than paying to replace the books. We have just got to become more organized around here.

By the way, I just read an article about really icky bacteria and viruses in pools and ponds. Make sure not to swallow any water from the pond or pool, especially if any of your bunkmates have had diarrhea. I'd hate for you to end up in the infirmary again.

Tonight Dad and I are going to watch something on the History Channel about the origins of the Serbian-Croatian conflict. Dad is such a history buff! In my next letter I'll share the highlights of the show.

I miss you so much!

Love,

Mom

After reviewing both letters, I decided to send the second version, just to be safe. I didn't want to puncture any illusions our sons had about their Dad and me and the predictable life they think we lead, or to have them worry that we were turning into DVD wastrels. After all, parents have a right to keep some secrets from their kids, don't they?

Can I Have S'More Vacation, Please?

We knew it was time to pack up and return home from our family vacation when we ran out of marshmallows and graham crackers. Making s'mores had been our main source of entertainment every night during the trip, and frankly, we had no backup plan. This was not my fault. I had packed enough chocolate to last half the population of Zurich for a month, but the individual in our party (whom I shall not name, as she is a minor child) in charge of packing the marshmallows and graham crackers had miscalculated badly, thus aborting our trip. It was a shame, really, since leaving after only three days meant that I had logged more hours planning this last fling of summer than we spent on the actual trip itself. Besides, I had gotten used to the novel sensation of being relaxed, and I liked it.

Still, my crack investigative skills had paid off. We ended up at a beautiful location, a rustic canyon retreat boasting clean cabins—and maid service! This is as close as I like to get to roughing it. After all, "rustic" can be code for "Can you help me get the Sterno going here? And shoo those bears away before they eat all the hot dogs!" I love nature, but I also love it from the safe distance of a room that can be locked at night. As a kid, I was forced on several occasions to have close encounters with nature in a sleeping bag under the stars. While the stars were beautiful and bounteous, sleeping on rocky ground left much to be desired, namely, sleep. Besides, who wants to sleep in a bag? I suspect I am averse to camping out because I am Jewish, but hey, if your ancestors had spent forty years wandering in a desert without maid service, indoor plumbing or Chinese takeout, you'd prefer vacationing at the closest Radisson, too.

Our cabins had no TVs or computer access, a fact that I kept secret from the kids until we were firmly ensconced there and it was too late for them to refuse to come along. Our main activity for the first hour was giving our lungs, filled with high-octane Los Angeles "air," a chance to receive a transfusion of clean, fresh air, scented faintly with eucalyptus. This was utterly exhausting, leaving us only enough energy for a mild stroll through the campgrounds. Walking through the area, we saw things quite foreign to urban dwellers: woodpeckers, scrub jays, hares, and other astonishingly beautiful and amazingly diverse creations.

Like most other guests at this retreat, we dined at a picnic table outside our cabin by the light of the fire we built in our individual fire pits. After dinner, we got down to the serious business of making s'mores. I hoped that the novelty of roasting marshmallows over an open fire might dim the pain our boys felt not knowing know who was ahead in the eighth inning of a critical game in the National League, as there was no ESPN reception for at least thirty miles around. But it was hard going for them, finding themselves stuck with parents determined to help them appreciate the wonders of nature at a pricey bucolic cabin geared to Yuppie types who have no clue how to pitch a tent.

When conversation began to lag, I was gobsmacked by a brilliant idea.

"Hey everybody, let's sing some camp songs!" I suggested. This notion would not have seemed so radical when the kids were tots and still thought everything I said was as brilliant as if God Himself had said it. But they were older now, and wiser.

"Uh, Mom, I don't think so," said one, looking around worriedly. What would the neighbors over at the next cabin think?

"Oh come on," I rejoined. "How often do we all get to sit around under the open skies like this, rusticating and roasting marshmallows?"

I ignored their desperate pleas that I not sing, even when they vowed to forego allowance for six months. They really, passionately, did not want me to sing. But they were too late. The spirit had moved me, or perhaps it had just been the smoke of the campfire blowing in my face, but I threw my arm around one kid and sang out, "Someone's singing lord, kumbaya; Someone's singing lord, kumbaya . . . ."

"Excuse me, lady, I'm not your kid," said the kid whom I had embraced, quickly disengaging from me. Well, who could tell? It was dark out there, and the kid had snuck over from another picnic table to insinuate herself into our graham crackers. I didn't think it was so unreasonable to expect her to sing for her after-supper s'mores.

"Mom, you're embarrassing us," a pre-teen said in his most urgent tone.

Meanwhile, the kid I embraced ran away with her marshmallow on a twig still *en flambé*. My husband sat contentedly, sipping a Scotch and trying not to look smug as he watched our neighbor ineffectually poking at the dying embers of his fire. My husband took great pride in having devoted a full half hour to preparing the kindling, to ensure a roaring, long-lasting flame.

"Just give it a try," I said. "Be open to new ideas. Come

on, everyone! 'Someone's singing lord, kumbaya; Oh lord, kumbaya . . . .'"

"What a dumb song!" my daughter said. "Did they run out of words other than 'kumbaya'? And what does kumbaya mean, anyway?"

She had a point. What did kumbaya mean, anyway, and why did everyone sing it, especially Democrats?

"If you'd only learn to just sit back and enjoy some single-malt Scotch with me, you wouldn't feel the need to sing," my husband observed.

I was not yet willing to concede defeat. "When you're down . . . and troubled . . . and you need a helping hand . . . ." I closed my eyes and sang in a wobbly voice, jetting my emotional self back thirty years. When I opened my eyes during the next stanza, I discovered our picnic table had been depopulated. Only I remained, along with my husband, who was calmly replenishing his cup with Scotch.

"Where'd everybody go?" I asked. The kids had vanished, but I spied one hiding behind a nearby tree. I had warned him that he would one day regret choosing fire engine red sneakers, but of course he didn't listen.

I got up from our table and went on a search. Two kids were sitting with other families, trying to blend in. Another was going from table to table, desperately seeking news about the Dodgers. They all pretended they had never seen me before in their short, tax-dependent status lives.

The next day, keeping in the spirit of wholesome, family-friendly activities, I announced it was time to hike one of the canyon trails. None of the kids was willing to go.

"There's a sign at the trail warning that this is the natural habitat of rattlesnakes, bobcats and mountain lions," protested one child. "No way am I going."

"I see," I said. "You're afraid for your own life, but you don't mind if Dad and I go?"

"I can't impose my values on the two of you," he said, reading the sports section of a newspaper he had borrowed from a neighbor.

We left our kids to their own devices, which meant they would just lie around the cabin, pining away for civilization, while we headed for the trail. The trail was narrow, and I took the lead.

"What were we supposed to do if we saw a mountain lion?" I asked. Flyers at the entrance to the retreat instructed us on the proper etiquette during unplanned meetings with some of God's creatures who could, should they so choose, tear you from limb to limb.

"If it's a mountain lion, we look it straight in the eye, speak calmly yet firmly, and remind it we carry only $20 in cash at any given time."

"Okay, but what if it's a bobcat?"

"I don't remember. We'll just hope it thinks it's a mountain lion."

The trail snaked higher and higher, and I was not sure whether my heart was pumping faster from exertion or fear. What if we did see a rattler? What if we saw a mountain lion and spoke firmly yet calmly, reminded it we only had $20 in cash, and it tore us apart anyway? Whose stupid idea was this, to come to such a dangerous place? Along the trail we spotted our kids far below, happily lolling around in the pool. We shouted and waved to them, our voices echoing down through the canyon. I hoped it would not be the last time we would ever see our children again, but I was beginning to wonder how this ever-narrowing and winding trail could get us back down to the canyon and the cabins.

"Say, why am I in front here? If we do encounter a wild animal, I want you to do the talking," I said.

"Don't worry. Don't you trust me?"

I wondered how many women, secretly despised by their husbands or boyfriends, had heard words just like this from the men they loved. I thought about how easy it would be to suggest a hike like this to someone you wanted to knock off. It would just take a little push at an opportune moment, and presto! The spurned woman would be thrown over, both literally and figuratively. Perhaps the altitude had begun to affect my judgment, but I began to question the security of my own marriage.

"Do you really love me?" I asked.

"Do you have to ask?"

"As a matter of fact, I do."

"Yes, I love you," my husband said.

"Then get me down from this mountain!" I shouted.

"Stop shouting or you'll scare the animals! Anyway, we're making our way down and so far the only wildlife we've seen are some squirrels. I was hoping I could save you from a bobcat. Wouldn't that be a great story to tell our kids and grandkids one day?"

"At this point I'll settle for telling our kids and grandkids that we hiked for miles up a mountain that is the natural habitat of natural born killers and we emerged alive and well," I said.

Eventually, we ended up on somebody's farm and trekked back to our canyon cabin, passing more woodpeckers and scrub jays. I was deliriously happy to see them.

That night, after dinner, I still couldn't quite manage to get the entire family to sing "If I Had a Hammer," but when I used the last of the marshmallows as ransom, at least I got them to hum a few bars.

Look Ma, No Hands!

For weeks, I had been plagued with worrisome and mysterious health ills. As usual, I encouraged my imagination to run riot, and envisioned some dreadful malady attacking my innocent self. To confirm my own diagnosis, I paid a visit to Luciann, my trusty nurse practitioner.

"What brings you here today?" she asked.

"I'm a wreck, Luciann. I can't sleep at night. My stomach's in knots. I've got constant indigestion, heart palpitations, and my left eyelid keeps twitching. Also, I can't seem to stop biting my lower lip."

Luciann dutifully wrote this down in my chart.

"Hmm," she said, mulling the information over and tapping her pen on my chart. "You have teens, don't you?"

"Yes, two. Plus another two in training."

"Any of them driving?"

"How did you know?" Luciann never failed to amaze me with her perceptive powers of diagnosis.

"These are classic symptoms of *teenasaurus legalis motoritis*," Luciann said. "When teens begin to drive, parents are literally booted out of the driver's seat. This creates tremendous emotional conflict, and often convulses the body with fear. After all, everyone knows that teens are lousy drivers. If you have a teen driver, I'm pretty sure that's what you're experiencing."

Luciann was right. My symptoms *had* kicked in shortly after our eldest son received his driver's permit and after his formal driving lessons ended. This left me or my husband to have the white-knuckle opportunity of being the passenger while he navigated our 3,000-pound minivan down city streets.

"Is there any treatment?" I asked. "I'm sentenced to a minimum of thirty more hours of practice with him before he gets his license. I don't know if I can take it."

"Unfortunately, medical science hasn't come up with anything for this condition. I could prescribe an antidepressant, but you probably won't want to nod off while your kid is behind the wheel. You can try some antacids for the indigestion, but you'll have to just ride it out, pardon the pun. However, I'm giving you a referral to a good plastic surgeon. You'll probably want to see about restoring that bottom lip."

Luciann assured me that *teenasaurus legalis motoritis* was rarely fatal, but I still wasn't sure how I'd survive it. It also astounded me that kids still in the throes of acne were deemed responsible enough to drive. Half these kids can't even remember to close a refrigerator door when they leave the kitchen, yet they are entrusted with the enormous responsibility of driving a motor vehicle, most likely while yakking on a cell phone at the same time.

Perhaps in the distant past, when kids had to shoulder serious work on the family farm, sixteen was not too young to learn to navigate automobiles. But these days, when a kid's idea of responsibility involves uploading new photos of himself on his personal Web site, I worry.

At least we managed to wait till our son was seventeen before he had serious grip time on a steering wheel. This was not simply gritty parental determination on our part to forestall this new, terrifying epoch in parenthood. It was also because the cost of insuring a 16-year-old boy in Los Angeles could have paid for a private taxi to shuttle him anywhere he wanted for a year. The insurance was staggeringly unaffordable—thank God. But after months of research, during which our son inevitably became seventeen, we found a company that would insure him without forcing us to take out a second mortgage.

We started with small, seemingly safe little drives in the neighborhood. Nothing fancy, like backing out of the driveway or parallel parking, just basic moves going forward, as well as stopping, turning, and signaling. I vowed to be calm.

"TURN THE WHEEL TO THE LEFT!" I shrieked, as he threatened to peel the paint off another car next to us.

"Calm down, Mom! I saw it!" my son said. "You're also tearing the leather out of the armrest."

I tried to slow my breathing and willed my hair to stop falling out, but stress can be brutal on the system. This is especially true when your kid is jabbing the gas pedal spasmodically, lurching you forward haphazardly, like on a roller coaster before the drop.

"SLOW DOWN!" I shouted, even though, in fairness, he had plenty of time to stop at the red light. Did he see it was a red light?

"Mom! I know what I'm doing!"

I know what I'm doing. Whenever a teenager says this to a parent, the parent laughs maniacally inside. These are terrifying words.

At a four-way stop sign, we inched out so slowly that another driver gestured rudely at us and honked his horn. "Ignore nasty people who honk their horns at you or try to rattle you," I advised. "Just continue to drive the way you know is safe. TURN THE WHEEL TO THE RIGHT! YOU'RE GOING TO HIT THAT CAR!"

"I'm not going to hit the car! I saw it! Now you're the one rattling me. And can you stop with all the sound effects? You're freaking me out."

He had a point. I had been gasping in terror approximately every three seconds. It sounded unseemly, and I vowed to try to stay saner. Maybe that antidepressant wasn't such a bad idea after all. On the other hand, there were some unexpected side benefits to my situation. During Pilates class, for example, the teacher always nags me to hold my ab muscles tight while performing many other bodily contortions. But with my teen at the wheel, tight abs result effortlessly. In fact, if they were any tighter they'd be marble.

Eventually, we completed a two-mile circuit of the neighborhood, and my son did a respectable job of pulling into the driveway. No injuries were reported.

Back in the house, however, I popped a migraine pill and put myself to bed to recover. Our excursion had taken only ten minutes, but it felt like hours. Getting through another thirty hours of this was going to be one of the hardest things I'd ever have to do in my life.

Undaunted by my paranoia, my son asked for more driving time the next day. "How else will I pass my driving test unless I get more practice?" he asked.

This time, the younger kids wanted to come with us. It seemed like a better adventure than emptying out the freezer, digging for ice cream sandwiches hidden behind old packages of peas and corn. It wasn't enough that my son was endangering his life and my own; now he had the opportunity to endanger his siblings as well. Everyone piled in the car, including our dog, Ken. He hates being left alone at home.

Our adventure began with backing out of the driveway, a tricky maneuver because our street is narrow and cars are usually hogging valuable space directly across the street. I really tried to keep my mouth shut as much as possible and to minimize my distracting sound effects. This lasted about eighteen seconds.

"Wait! You're in reverse! You've got to turn the wheel LEFT to make the car go right!" I wasn't sure what an ulcer felt like, but I was sure I had just spiked one on the spot. My fingernails found their familiar grooves in the armrest and dug in for dear life.

Out on the street, my youngest son sensed that this was not just any old car ride with no purpose: This promised to be a journey of thrills, suspense and danger with no purpose.

"Floor it!" he urged his brother, while I shot him a warning look. I knew he couldn't wait to become old enough to sit in this same driver's seat, while getting his own chance to whack four years off my life.

"Do you have a good collision rider on your insurance, Mom?" asked my middle son, who is cautious by nature.

My daughter remained uncharacteristically quiet in the back seat, while Ken, perhaps sensing peril, began to shed copiously.

"When can we go on the freeway?" my newbie driver asked, hurtling us forward toward a major intersection.

"BEGIN TO MAKE YOUR TURN NOW!" I gasped, convinced that none of the other drivers on the boulevard were aware of our existence.

"That was fun!" my youngest boy said. "When I drive, I'll go a lot faster than this." I vowed at that moment that he won't drive till he's at least twenty-six.

My son piloted us to a shopping mall three miles from home, maneuvering around a narrow circular ramp and parking squarely between the lines of his parking spot. We all admired the execution. Mission accomplished, we headed back home.

This driver's education has taught me a thing or two. In particular, I realize that with three more future drivers under my roof, I need to shore up my fraying nerves. I'm thinking skydiving, bungee-jumping, and invigorating activities of that nature ought to do the trick. And by then I probably will have earned those abs of marble.

My Two Papas

More than almost anything else in his life, my Papa loved a good cigar and a good laugh. When I was a little girl, Papa, my father's father, would regale me with his exploits of practical jokes he deployed against unsuspecting victims. This was more than a mere hobby. The man was on a mission to bemuse, befuddle, embarrass and sometimes even annoy with intended irony.

One evening, at an elegant home where my grandparents were dinner guests, Papa surreptitiously placed an array of drugstore remedies for stomach upset along the gleaming dining room table. My grandmother burned with shame and anger at her prankster husband, but Papa was hugely satisfied with the uproar he caused. Needless to say, my grandparents were never invited back. And while traveling in Europe, during an era when it was still the custom to set one's shoes outside the hotel room for the staff to shine, Papa woke up extra early to switch everyone's shoes around.

Papa was equally irreverent when it came to religion. When he was only seven, his father died, leaving his mother and six siblings nearly penniless. A rabbi, meaning to offer comfort, told my grandfather that his father's death was God's will. But my grandfather's early childhood had lacked the spiritual foundation for this remark to have made any sense, or to have offered anything but cold comfort. Words can hurt and words can heal. These powerful, un-intentionally painful words prompted this seven-year-old boy to re-nounce God for good. Stubborn to the core, he never looked back.

Although Judaism forbids cremation, Papa paid no heed to that any more than he did to the prohibition against eating ham. While puffing on a Dutch Master's cigar, he told us with a twinkle in his eye that when the time came, we had better be careful not to mix up his ashes with those of his beloved cigars.

My mother's father, my Zeyde, could not have been more different from Papa. Born in Poland to an Orthodox family, he es-caped from the Polish army during World War I. His deliverance came unexpectedly: Zeyde carried with him a volume of poetry, whose work was much admired by an army superior. He gladly exchanged the volume for his freedom. He eventually made it to America, determined to live according to Jewish values, but with a modern spin. Like so many other immigrants of his generation, he discarded some traditions of Jewish life that had fortified his life in Europe. In America, he embraced Conservative Judaism, a sect that tried to ride the middle of the road between Orthodoxy and Reform, and became ordained as a rabbi in their movement. He and my grandmother may have been "greenhorns," but they were determined that their children wouldn't be.

Zeyde was as somber as Papa was mischievous, and his life revolved around studying, teaching, establishing Jewish schools and congregations, and performing life cycle rites for the members of the congregations he served throughout the United States. Like many clergymen, he had to pack up and move frequently to find work. He served congregations in Pittsburgh, Pennsylvania; Wheeling, West Virginia; Corpus Christi, Texas (we always loved the irony of that) and, only a touch less ironic, Las Vegas, Nevada, where Papa's claim to fame was hitching Elizabeth Taylor and Eddie Fisher for however long that union lasted. I doubt that he was ever found near a slot machine.

Zeyde had a keen intellect, but he rarely laughed at the jokes we told at family dinners, and had little use for entertainment. "A *vaste* of time!" he would say if he saw us watching television (although he was spot on about that). The brightest smiles I ever saw on his handsome, intelligent face always arose from seeing his children and grandchildren. To their credit, both Papa and Zeyde worked to keep the family peace by refraining—most of the time—from insulting one another's religion or apostasy.

Growing up, I felt enormously lucky to have such wildly divergent grandfathers. The world seemed bigger and broader because of them, and as opposite as they were, I loved them both very much. I wasn't sure whose model I'd follow religiously. There was something sacred about Zeyde solemnly reciting the Hebrew Kiddush over the Sabbath wine on Friday night, something that connected me to thousands of years of Jewish history and to my ancestors. But Papa's audacious style was irresistibly fun: He'd raise a wine glass in front of company and announce mirthfully, "Here's to those who wish me well, and all the rest can go to hell!"

Truthfully, Zeyde's seriousness kept me from thinking that I could ever be as religious as he was. He didn't mean to, but Zeyde conveyed the message that humor and spirituality were as mismatched as Papa's hotel shoes. I admired his commitment to Jewish values, but let's face it: He wasn't the life of the party, he was the life of the library. Papa, on the other hand, had endeared us all with his humor, though it may have masked great personal pain.

When I began to explore traditional Judaism, I was happily surprised to hear Orthodox rabbis, complete with beards and sometimes even black hats, cracking great one-liners during their sermons or classes. This was a revelation that hadn't come down from

Mount Sinai: It wasn't only secular Jews like Woody Allen and Billy Crystal who were hilarious. Religious Jews could be funny, too!

As a beginning writer I was irresistibly drawn to humor. Absurdities of life abounded, and I was eager to poke fun at them. I was thrilled to discover that my work could make people laugh (though I also quickly learned that my work would sometimes offend). Laughter, as Papa knew so well, was a survival tool in a world of pain and trouble. But Zeyde understood something, too, which was that when the joke ended and the laughter died down, you needed a spiritual anchor, a roadmap for living.

My grandfathers are both long gone, but I cherish the gifts they each provided. I hope that they each might finally share a laugh together and call it even that their granddaughter grew up to believe in God—and in humor.

About Judy Gruen

Judy Gruen has crafted a career of writing sophisticated, relatable yet clean humor, earning her a loyal following of readers for her Web-based column "Off My Noodle," published on www.judygruen.com. Her essays have appeared in *Ladies' Home Journal, Woman's Day, Family Circle, The Chicago Tribune*, and many other newspapers across the U.S. and Canada. A frequent contributor to the *Los Angeles Jewish Journal*, Judy's audioblog, "Just Off My Noodle," is broadcast on OURadio.org.

Her first book, *Carpool Tunnel Syndrome: Motherhood as Shuttle Diplomacy*, earned a merit award for humor from the Midwest Independent Publishers' Association, and was excerpted in *Woman's Day*. Her second book, *Till We Eat Again: Confessions of a Diet Dropout*, was named best humor book of 2003 by the Midwest Independent Publishers Association. It was also serialized on eDiets.com's "eDiets Extra" newsletter, sent to more than 3 million subscribers. Her humor has been anthologized in five books.

Judy is a member of the National Society of Newspaper Columnists, The Association for Applied and Therapeutic Humor, and the Authors Guild. She lives in Los Angeles with her husband, four children and friendly dog.